doggy
FASHION

doggy FASHION

ALISON JENKINS

BARRON'S

First edition for the United States, its territories
and dependencies, and Canada published in 2003
by Barron's Educational Series, Inc.

This book was conceived,
designed, and produced by
THE IVY PRESS LIMITED
The Old Candlemakers
West Street, Lewes
East Sussex BN7 2NZ, U.K.

Creative Director PETER BRIDGEWATER
Publisher SOPHIE COLLINS
Editorial Director STEVE LUCK
Senior Project Editor CAROLINE EARLE
Art Director CLARE BARBER
Design Manager TONY SEDDON
Designer JANE LANAWAY
Photographer CALVEY TAYLOR-HAW
Picture Researcher VANESSA FLETCHER

All inquiries should be addressed to:
Barron's Educational Series, Inc.
250 Wireless Blvd.
Hauppauge, NY 11788
www.barronseduc.com

International Standard Book No.: 0-7641-2584-2

Library of Congress Catalog No.: 2002116529

Printed and bound in China

9 8 7 6 5 4 3 2 1

contents

Introduction

to dressing up

Doggy Fashion is all about creating fancy-dress costumes for canine companions who like life to have a little glamour. I can assure you a great deal of fun and laughter was had by all concerned—the dogs involved adored their 15 minutes of fame and the doggy treats, too.

I've got teeth and attitude—I'll only do it if I can have the Space Dog outfit!

If your pooch has loads of personality and likes to party, then this is definitely the book for you. If you're hosting a special get-together for friends or family (the canine variety included, of course), or if you're staging a photo session for the family album, a well-styled costume can be just the thing to add a touch of humor while including the family pet. No dog need be a plain old hound dog, we've got it all here—classic style, glamour, and humor, along with a decent helping of good old rock 'n' roll to finish.

Look to the end of the book and you'll see all the patterns printed on graph paper, so that you can scale them up to suit your dog. For added ease when dressing up and quick release when the dressing's done, all the costumes have hook-and-loop (velcro) fastenings at the center back. And we've got all the accessories, too!

Now if you're wondering: how much have the canine couture-wearers enjoyed themselves and exactly how much have they been coerced into doing, I can assure you now: leave those worries at the door. All the costumes in this book have been carefully designed to fit comfortably around canine anatomy and are easy to get in and out of. Our models are all well-loved pets and their owners were with them throughout the session to make sure no dog did what he or she did not want to do, and even they expressed surprise at some of the results. These dogs, each very different in character, all loved the dressing up, and took a lively interest in the camera. However, if your own dear dogs are of a more serious bent, please don't force them to dress up against their will. If you are not sure, try them out gently with a cut-down T-shirt; you never know—you may release their inner thespian.

I hope you'll have as much fun dressing up your canine friends in *Doggy Fashion* as we did with ours.

Millie experiences "celebrity exhaustion" now that her 15 minutes of fame are over.

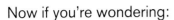

Sewing Basics

Understanding the fundamentals

The following pages will describe how to put all the doggy fashions together, so you can understand the fundamentals of cutting out, sewing, construction, and so on. Only very basic sewing skills are required, so don't panic if needlework isn't your specialty.

Scaling up patterns and cutting out

The patterns for each costume are printed to scale on a grid pattern on pages 100–123.

The first step is to draw the pattern to full size to fit your dog's measurements (*see page 100* for the dog-measuring guide). All you'll need to do this is a few sheets of blank paper to draw your own grid or dressmakers' pattern paper, which normally comes printed in 1-in. (2.5-cm) squares. Simply copy the templates onto your chosen grid, square for square. For medium-size dogs you need to use 2-in. (5-cm) squares, so you can use dressmaker's pattern paper, but for small or large dogs, it will be easier to draw your own grid for scaling up on plain paper. (*See the full instructions on page 100.*) You'll also need a pencil, a ruler, and a pair of paper-cutting scissors.

Small dog Use 1 1/2-in. (3.5-cm) squares.
Medium dog Use 2-in. (5-cm) squares.
Large dog Use 2 1/2-in. (6.5-cm) squares.

Chest measurements are approximately as follows:
Small dog under 20 in. (50 cm) chest.
Medium dog between 20 in. (50 cm) and 28 in. (70 cm) chest.
Large dog between 28 in. (70 cm) and 36 in. (90 cm) chest.

Simply draw the pattern on your sheet of dressmakers' pattern paper/scaled-up grid to match the pattern on the relevant template page. Make pencil dots where the pattern lines cross the lines on the graph, then join the dots to make the pattern (*see step 1 on page 12*). Make sure that you transfer any other important information on the template, e.g., notches, large dots, center lines, to your full-scale pattern.

The next step is cutting out. Each pattern page has a cutting plan that tells you how many of each pattern piece to cut in fabric, interfacing, etc. Fold your material in half, placing the selvages (the finished edges) together and with right sides facing each other, then place it flat on your work surface with the fold running down the left-hand side. Now, place the pattern pieces on the fabric

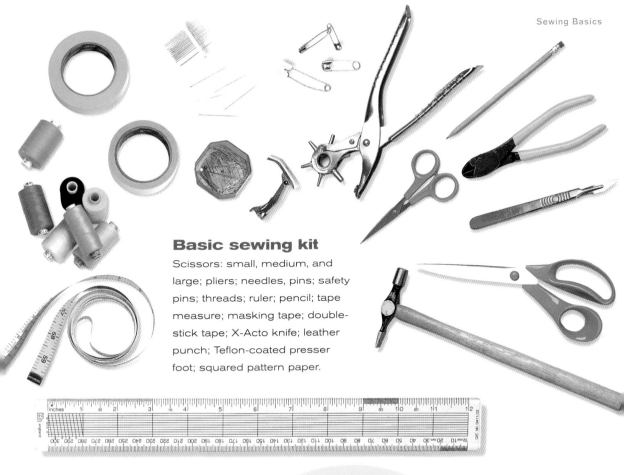

Basic sewing kit

Scissors: small, medium, and large; pliers; needles, pins; safety pins; threads; ruler; pencil; tape measure; masking tape; double-stick tape; X-Acto knife; leather punch; Teflon-coated presser foot; squared pattern paper.

with center lines on the fold, if necessary, and matching the straight of grain (*see note below*). Pin in place, then cut out using large, sharp dressmaking shears, keeping as close to the pattern edge as you can.

Note Woven fabrics have vertical threads (warp) and horizontal threads (weft). These form the straight lengthwise and crosswise grain of the fabric. In this book "straight of grain" always means the lengthwise grain. The straight-of-grain line on the pattern must be placed along the warp of the fabric. The fairy dog costume (*pages 48–53*) requires a "bias" strip to bind the waistline, cut diagonally across the fabric for maximum stretch.

I simply refuse to get out of my basket for less than $200 a day!

Pattern adjustments

Dogs, like humans, come in all shapes and sizes but, like humans, they conform to the same basic design. Make a note of your dog's basic measurements: chest, waist, leg lengths, back of neck to base of tail, back of neck to waist, and circumference of head. You'll know just by looking at him or her which category your dog falls into—small, medium, large—but you'll have to refer to the dog's own measurements for the fine-tuning. Lengthening and shortening pattern bodices or sleeves can easily be done either by folding the pattern or by adding an extra strip (*see step 3, page 12*). The chest size can be increased by adding a little to the side seam of the front and back bodice. Take the chest measurement from the pattern, and compare to the actual chest measurement; now divide the difference by 4 and add this to the front and back side seam. Remember, though, to add the same measurement to the sleeve seams to match. For the waist, simply add or take away the amount required from the pattern piece.

Measurements

Note that both standard and metric measurements are given in this book. The conversions are not exact, so use one set or the other. Fabric quantities given with the projects are for a medium-size dog.

Basic construction

Simplicity is key here; most of the costumes have very few pattern pieces (with the exception of Rock 'n' Roll Hero, *see page 92*), usually front, back, sleeves, and possibly a collar or facings. In general the construction procedure for each costume goes like this:

1. Join the shoulder and side seams.

2. Apply fastenings to the center back or front openings.

3. Apply collars and finish edges.

4. Join sleeve seams and insert into the armholes.

5. Add finishing touches such as buttons, topstitching, and decorations.

Plain, open seams are used throughout to join garment pieces together. The fabric should be placed right sides together and with the raw edges matching, and the sewing line (machine or hand) should be approximately $1/2$ in. (1.5 cm) in from the raw edge. Unless otherwise instructed, use this method (*see step 1, page 14*). Press all seams open except armholes and necklines.

Terms and phrases

As you read through the instructions you will find that several phrases come up quite frequently. Here are brief explanations.

Join stitch A seam to join two garment pieces together, taking the stated seam allowance.

With right sides facing Place the right side of both fabric pieces facing each other.

Seam allowance Usually ½ in. (1.5 cm)—the area between the stitching line and the raw edge.

Fuse interfacing Apply the interfacing, adhesive side down, to the wrong side of the fabric piece, then press using a steam iron. The heat and moisture cause the adhesive to melt and stick the interfacing to the fabric. Each pattern suggests the weight of interfacing to use for the required level of stiffness.

Reduce seam allowance Trim the seam allowance down to the suggested amount to reduce bulk inside a collar or facing.

Clip seam allowance Make small clips or snips into the trimmed seam allowance around a curve. This allows the edge to lie flat when pressed or turned right side out.

Fold and stitch Usually for hems or front or back openings. Simply fold the specified amount along a raw edge, either once or twice as per instructions, then machine-stitch as directed for a hem, a casing, or an opening.

Undercollar/top collar Collars are usually cut in two pieces or in one piece that is folded in half lengthwise. Interfacing is always fused to the wrong side of the undercollar, and that, in turn, is the side that is applied to the neckline first. The top collar is left unstiffened.

Underlap/overlap This applies to openings both front and back. It is up to you which way you want to do this—right over left or left over right. Hook-and-loop tape and snaps must be applied to the underside of the overlap and the upper side of the underlap.

Rolie wanted a change from her usual little black dress—pink, pink, pink, and lots of froth!

Patterns and cutting out

When making a garment, accuracy in pattern-making and cutting out is important. Care taken at this stage will save you headaches later on!

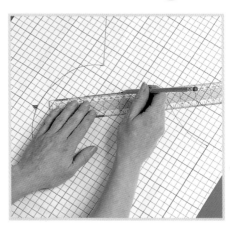

① Copy the templates on the pattern paper, placing them on the main grid as they are on the page. Mark a dot on your paper where the pattern lines cross a grid line. Join the dots, using a ruler; sketch curves freehand. Transfer pattern marks, such as fold lines and notches.

② Always fold fabric in half with the selvages together and the right sides facing unless otherwise stated. Place the pattern pieces on the fold where indicated, and make sure that they lie exactly on the straight of grain. Cut out the pieces carefully, using sharp dressmaking scissors, keeping as close to the edge of the pattern paper as you can, and taking extra care around curved armholes and necklines.

③ To lengthen a pattern piece, simply cut horizontally across one side to the other. Using the dog's own measurements, calculate how much the adjustment should be. Now cut a strip of paper a little wider than the pattern piece and a little longer than the adjustment measurement. Place the pattern pieces on the strip, allowing a gap the correct size between the cut edges. Use masking tape to secure the paper, and trim the side edges to match the line of the original pattern.

④ Shortening a pattern follows the same principle but in reverse; instead of adding to the original pattern, you'll be taking away. This time draw a horizontal line across the pattern from one side to the other using a pencil and a ruler. Calculate the adjustment from the dog's measurement as before. Now make a sharp pleat along the pencil line, the width of the adjustment measurement. Use tabs of masking tape to hold the pleat securely. Trim the side edges neatly to follow the line of the original pattern, if necessary.

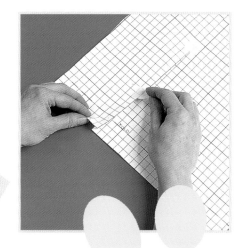

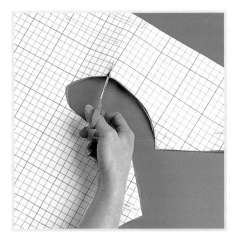

SEWING TIP

When clipping into the fabric to indicate notches or center lines, cut only halfway across the 1/2 in. (1.5 cm) seam allowance. Otherwise the seam or edge will fray.

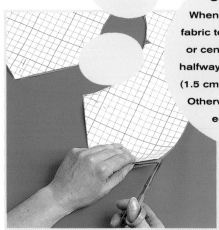

⑤ After you have cut out all the pattern pieces it is important to transfer any notches, fold lines, or other marks that will help you during the construction of the costume. For example, the notches on the front and back armholes are very important; these points mark the position of the sleeve seam and the center of the sleeve cap. Simply make a small clip into the seam allowance at this point using sharp embroidery scissors.

⑥ The center line is another important point to mark. If this is placed on a fold, place the point of the scissors in the fold of the fabric at the neck edge and make a small cut. When using patterns that have overlapping openings at the center, front, or back, mark both the center line and the fold of the overlap with small clips as before. Where necessary, fold the fabric, wrong sides together. Transfer the pattern marks to the fabric pieces.

Basic sewing and construction

In this book simple open seams are used. The edges of constructional seams have been left unfinished. Choose fabrics that don't fray easily. After stitching, press seams open.

1 Unless otherwise stated, all seams are stitched with the right sides of the pieces facing. The stitching line should be about ½ in. (1.5 cm) from the raw edge—use the guide on the sewing machine plate to keep it straight. For speed, pin the fabric pieces together with the pins at right angles to the raw edge. Alternatively, baste, as shown, using long running stitches.

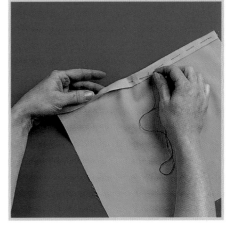

2 Lower edges look better when they are finished. The easiest way to do this is to fold a ³/8-in. (1-cm) or ½-in. (1.5-cm) hem along the edge, then repeat. Pin and stitch this double hem close to the inner fold.

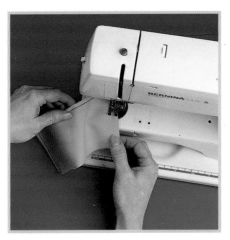

3 Topstitching adds a nice touch of professionalism to your dog's costume on edges, hems, collars, cuffs, and belts. It's quicker to do this by machine, but you can do it by hand using a small running stitch, perhaps with a contrasting decorative thread. Make the collar/cuff/belt, turn it right side out, and press. Now simply machine-stitch about ¼ in. (6 mm) away from the edge of the piece.

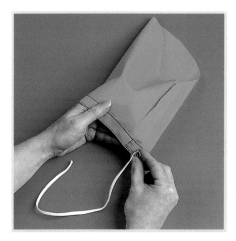

4 A casing is a way of finishing a raw edge at a cuff or ankle and also serves as a channel for elastic. Join the sleeve/leg seam and press it open. Fold and stitch a 1/2 in. (1.5 cm) double hem at the lower edge, stitching close to the inner fold and then along the folded edge. Unpick a few stitches of the sleeve seam between the two lines of stitching to create a small gap. Thread a length of elastic through the casing using a large safety pin. Stitch the ends of the elastic securely together. Form a gathered cuff/ankle.

5 Setting sleeves into an armhole can be a little tricky. Join the sleeve seam and finish the cuff edge, if necessary. Turn the bodice wrong side out, but have the sleeve right side out. Insert the sleeve, matching the sleeve seam to the notch on the front armhole and the center sleeve cap with the notch on the back armhole. Pin the sleeve in place; you may have to ease the sleeve a little into the armhole to make it fit smoothly. Baste, if necessary, and stitch in place.

6 Gathered sleeves are a much simpler operation. While the sleeve is flat, run a row of large machine-gathering stitches between the dots on the sleeve cap. Now assemble the sleeve as before, and pin it into the lower part of the armhole, leaving the sleeve cap free for the moment. Pull up the gathering stitches until the sleeve fits the armhole neatly. Pin, baste, and stitch in place.

Collars and cuffs

Collars, cuffs, and facings are a decorative and functional way of finishing a raw edge. In general, some form of fabric stiffening is required; iron-on interfacing is quick and easy to use.

1 Cut out collar/cuff/facing and iron-on interfacing as directed. Place the interfacing adhesive side down on the wrong side of the cut-out fabric piece. The adhesive is shiny, so you'll easily be able to tell the difference. Now fuse the interfacing to the fabric using a hot steam iron. The action of the steam and the heat causes the adhesive to melt and adhere to the fabric. The interfacing is fused to the undercollar section.

2 Fold the collar in half (for a one-piece collar/cuff), or place the two collar pieces together with right sides facing if it is in two pieces. Now pin or baste the ends together taking the usual 1/2-in. (1.5-cm) seam allowance, then machine-stitch. You will see that the neck edge has been left free (or, for a cuff, it would be the sleeve edge).

3 Reducing the seam allowance is necessary when turning collars, cuffs, or facings the right side out. If the seam allowance is left untrimmed at a pointed corner, the remaining bulk of the fabric would prevent a neat finish. Using small, sharp scissors, trim all seam allowances (except the neck edge) down to about 1/8 in. (3 mm), and clip diagonally across at the corners.

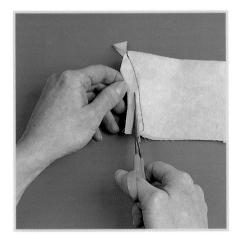

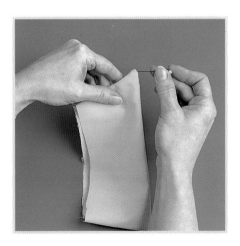

④ The piece can now be turned right side out. Use your fingers to push out any corners from the inside. For sharp points, use a "point turner" to tease out the fabric, but be careful not to pull too hard as the point may fray. You can also use a knitting needle or the pointed blades of a small pair of scissors for this; just poke gently from the inside.

SEWING TIP
Remember when using iron-on interfacing that it requires steam in addition to heat in order for the adhesive to fuse to the fabric.

⑤ It's time now to apply the piece to the main garment; a collar and bodice are shown here. Open up the neck edge of the collar, and pin the interfaced side (the undercollar) to the right side of the neckline edge. Remember to match the front and back of the collar to the center front and back of the bodice. Pin, baste, and stitch the collar in place.

⑥ Trim the seam allowance along the stitched neck edge, then clip along the raw edges so the curved seam will lie flat. Fold the seam allowance of the remaining raw edge of the collar to the inside, and press it flat with your fingers. Pin the fold to the neckline, enclosing any raw edges. Slipstitch it in place as shown, taking tiny stitches alternately through the fold and the neck edge.

Fastenings

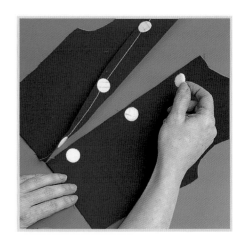

Fastenings have to be pretty secure to make sure the wriggling dog stays clothed! All the costumes have center-back openings, for easy dog dressing, and some have additional decorative front openings.

Hook-and-loop dots

For securing openings in lightweight fabrics, hook-and-loop dots are sufficient. Fold and press the overlap and underlap as directed along the center-back edges, then position the hook-and-loop fastener dots. Use the fluffy loop half of the hook-and-loop fastener for the underlap side and the thinner hook half for the overlap side. Now machine-stitch down the center of each dot, securing it and the folded edge at the same time.

Hook-and-loop tape

When using a heavier fabric, it's best to use hook-and-loop tape. Fold and press the edges of the bodice overlap and underlap as directed, then pin the loop side of the hook-and-loop tape to the underlap and the hook side to the overlap as before. Machine-stitch down each side of the hook-and-loop tape, using the machine's zipper foot, to secure it to the fabric.

Snap fasteners

These are easy alternatives to hook-and-loop dots, but suited to lightweight fabrics. Prepare the bodice as before, then position the fasteners as required. Use the top, or ball, half of the fastener on the overlap, since that has the flatter base, and the socket part on the underlap. Hand-sew each part in place securely.

Fabric ties

① A very attractive way to decorate or secure a garment at the center back or at the neckline. Cut two fabric strips to size, then press a ³⁄8-in. (1-cm) hem to the wrong side, across one short end and along both sides. You will need a pair of ties for each fastening.

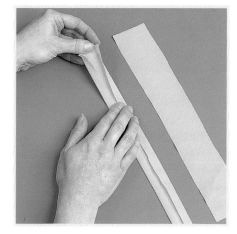

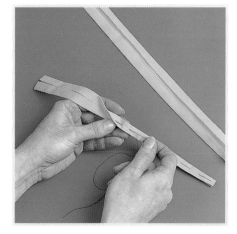

② Now fold the tie in half lengthwise, enclosing the raw edges. Machine-stitch the tie together close to the edge, across the short end and down one side. Stitch the remaining raw ends of the ties on each side of the garment opening.

Accessories!! Now you're talking my language!

Bands

① Bands for belts or hats can be made in a similar way. Cut a strip of fabric or mock leather to the size required, then position a strip of double-stick tape down the center on the wrong side. Peel the backing paper away from the tape. Fold both the long edges toward the center, and press them down firmly onto the adhesive surface of the tape. Thread the band through a decorative buckle.

Hat making

If you want to get ahead, get a hat! A fancy-dress costume can sometimes look unfinished without some sort of headgear. The following basic steps apply to all the hats in this book. Most hats consist of two basic parts: the brim and the crown—which may itself consist of a side and top section.

1 If the brim is wide or needs to stick out stiffly, it must be stiffened with a medium-to-heavyweight iron-on interfacing. Fuse the stiffening to one brim piece, then lay the other piece on top. Machine-stitch very close to the outer edge, then trim neatly if necessary.

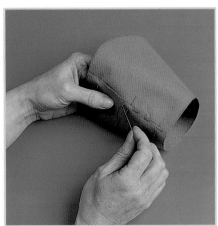

2 The crown side is a slightly curved strip that is joined to form (in most of the designs) a gently tapering cylinder. Felt is a good material for hat making because it does not fray, so seams can be overlapped instead of joined with right sides together, as for other constructional seams. Simply overlap the short (center back) edges by about 3/8-in. (1 cm), then machine-stitch—or sew by hand, if the hat is too small to fit under the presser foot.

3 The next step is to apply the crown top; this is usually a circular or oval-shaped piece that is stitched to the top edge of the crown side. Pin or baste the top to the side first, then stitch by machine or by hand, taking the smallest possible seam allowance.

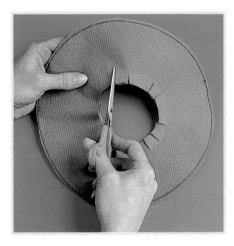

5 Place the crown over the brim so that the tabs around the inner edge sit up inside the lower edge of the crown. Now pin or baste the crown in place, then sew it securely by hand with small running stitches.

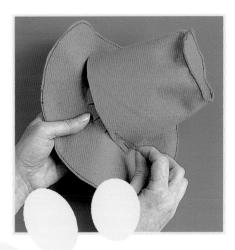

4 In order for the brim to fit the crown, the seam allowance around the inner edge must be clipped at regular intervals all the way around. Use small, sharp scissors for this, making each clip ½ in. (1.5 cm) long, forming little tabs all the way around. Bend each tab to sit at right angles to the hat brim.

SEWING TIP

As an alternative to iron-on interfacing for an extra-rigid hat brim, use double-stick adhesive stiffener used for making drape valances and tiebacks.

6 A hat, especially one for a dog, will not stay put all by itself! Cut a length of elastic just long enough to fit under the dog's chin snugly but not too tightly, then sew each end to the hat securely by hand. You could use ribbon ties as an alternative to this if you'd prefer a more decorative fastening.

Elvis, the King

nothin' but a hound dog...

Ladies and gemmen, we present . . . the King! No one ever threw a fancy-dress party without at least one Elvis in the building, did they? Here he is in the unforgettable Vegas years, cling-wrapped in his signature seventies jumpsuit, scintillating with fake jewels, a huge collar framing the face, and gold-framed megashades to complete the look. If you can get your doggy to wear a stylish Elvis wig, too, then go for it—if a costume's worth doing, it's worth overdoing! Choose a nice stretchy fabric to achieve the figure-hugging silhouette for which Elvis was notorious, and use glue to stick on the rhinestones (we used flat-backed cabochons) to avoid awkward hand sewing.

YOU WILL NEED
Basic sewing kit (*see pages 8–9*)

White stretch fabric 1 1/8 yd. (1 m)
Medium-weight iron-on interfacing 1/2 yd. (50 cm)

Dog Archie— more of a Jailhouse Elvis, really

5–8 hook-and-loop fastener dots white

Shades light and plastic only

Cabochons or rhinestones

Strong craft adhesive

YOU MIGHT NEED
Belt buckle not too heavy; for optional belt
Elvis wig if your dog is really into the look

method...

I've always been a sucker for rhinestones!

The Jumpsuit

1 Trace patterns given on page 101 to full size, and cut out pattern pieces in fabric and interfacing as directed. Join the two front sections along the center front up to the dot. Pin the two back pieces to the front at the shoulders; baste, as shown, and stitch. Fold a 1-in. (2.5-cm) hem down each side of the center back opening and baste in place.

2 Position hook-and-loop fastener dots at regular intervals along the folded edges—the loop side on the underlap and the hook side on the underside of the overlap, as shown. Machine-stitch down the center of the dots on both sides. Overlap the top (neck) edges of the center back by about 3/8 in. (1 cm), and secure with a few hand stitches.

③ Pin, baste, and machine-stitch the seams of both sleeves with right sides together. Fold a 3/8-in. (1-cm) double hem at the lower edge of each, opening out the sleeve seam flat as you go. Machine-stitch using a wide zigzag setting; this will serve as a decorative effect in addition to holding the hem in place.

NOTE

Elvis needs stretch fabric to achieve a figure-hugging silhouette, so use a small zigzag or stretch stitch on your machine when seaming or topstitching.

④ Turn both sleeves right side out, but keep the bodice wrong side out. Insert the sleeve into the armhole, matching the seam with the notch on the front armhole and the center of the sleeve cap with the notch on the back armhole.
Pin in place, baste, and machine-stitch. Insert the other sleeve in the same way.

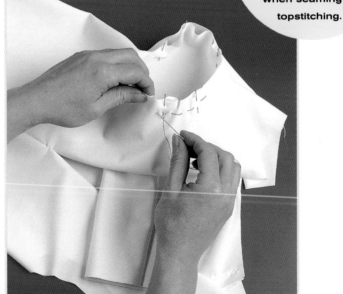

method...

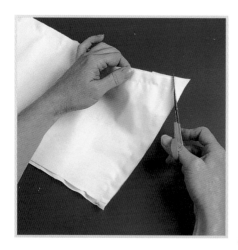

5 Fuse the interfacing collar piece to the wrong side of the undercollar. Pin the undercollar and top collar together, right sides facing; baste and stitch, leaving the neck edge free. Clip across the seam allowance at both collar tips, as shown, and trim the stitched edges to about 1/4 in. (6 mm).

6 Place the undercollar and back neck edges together with right sides facing and the center of the undercollar matching the overlapped center back opening. Pin, baste, as shown, and machine-stitch. Trim the seam allowances to about 1/4 in. (6 mm), and make a few small clips into the trimmed edge so that the seam will lie flat inside the collar when finished.

Bow wow WOW! Get me to Vegas right away!

7 Fold the seam allowance of the raw edge of the top collar to the wrong side, then pin the fold to the neckline, enclosing all the raw edges. Slipstitch the folded edge to the line of machine stitching, as shown, to finish the collar.

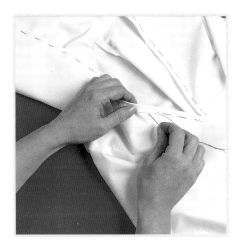

8 Fold the seam allowance on either side of the front opening to the inside, then pin or baste in place. Now topstitch the front opening and the collar, using a wide zigzag stitch setting, about $3/8$ in. (1 cm) away from the edge. As a decorative extra, why not use a contrasting metallic thread for the topstitching?

9 To complete Elvis's outfit, glue the jewel-colored cabochons in a symmetrical decorative design around the neckline and collar edge, using a strong, quick-drying craft adhesive. It is necessary to use a quick-drying, extra tacky adhesive because the cabochons are quite heavy and might slide out of position if you use an ordinary glue.

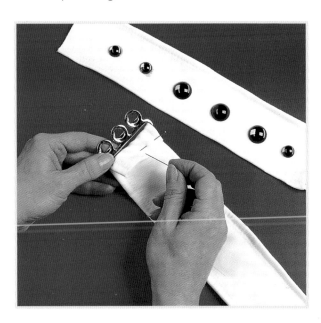

The Optional Belt

1 For the optional belt, cut two belt pieces, and fold in half lengthwise with right sides together. Stitch together down the long, raw edge, then turn right side out and topstitch close to both side edges. Slip one end of each piece through one side of the belt buckle, and secure with hand sewing. Glue on some cabochons. Stitch the free ends to the center back edges of the jumpsuit.

Pilgrim Father

because dogs can be Puritans, too...

Of course they had dogs on the *Mayflower*—can you imagine any self-respecting Pilgrim Father embarking (tee hee) on the treacherous voyage across the Atlantic from Plymouth, England to Plymouth, New England (and how lucky is that?), without his Best Friend? This fittingly somber little ensemble is made from black felt or from imitation suede, which is great because it doesn't fray, so that means no hemming, hurrah. It's the little details that make an outfit, so look for stylish buttons for the jacket and elegant buckles for the belt and hatband. Finish the crisp white neckline with a ribbon or tubing bow.

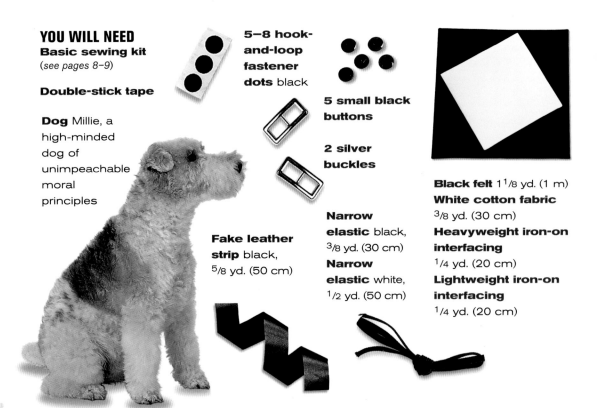

YOU WILL NEED

Basic sewing kit
(*see pages 8–9*)

Double-stick tape

Dog Millie, a high-minded dog of unimpeachable moral principles

5–8 hook-and-loop fastener dots black

5 small black buttons

2 silver buckles

Fake leather strip black, 5/8 yd. (50 cm)

Narrow elastic black, 3/8 yd. (30 cm)
Narrow elastic white, 1/2 yd. (50 cm)

Black felt 1 1/8 yd. (1 m)
White cotton fabric 3/8 yd. (30 cm)
Heavyweight iron-on interfacing 1/4 yd. (20 cm)
Lightweight iron-on interfacing 1/4 yd. (20 cm)

method...

The Frocked Waistcoat

1 Trace the patterns given on pages 102–103 to full size, and cut out pattern pieces as directed. Overlap the front edges, matching the center front lines. Pin in place, then machine-stitch together along the center line. Take five small buttons and position them an equal distance apart along the stitching line. Use double thread to hand-sew the buttons in place. If you have a button-stitching foot, you can secure the buttons using a sewing machine.

2 Keeping the waistcoat flat in front of you, place the four flaps along the lower edge, with their narrower top edges tucked about 3/8 in. (1 cm) under it. Space the flaps so their lower edges do not overlap each other and so that the back flaps are about 2 in. (5 cm) in from the center back edge. Baste them in place, as shown, and machine-stitch.

Gee, I'm dog-tired—
modeling is so exhausting.
Time for a quick nap.

3 To secure the center back opening, sew the loop side of the hook-and-loop-fastener dots to the underlap and the hook side to the underside of the overlap. The felt fabric does not fray, so there is no need to fold the seam allowance back first. Pin and machine-stitch both shoulder seams with right sides facing, then press the seams open.

4 Fuse the lightweight interfacing to the wrong side of the two undercollars. Pin the undercollars to the top collars with right sides facing, and machine-stitch around the outer edge, leaving the neck edge free. Using small, sharp scissors, cut diagonally across the seam allowance at each corner, then reduce the remaining seam allowance to about 1/8 in. (3 mm).

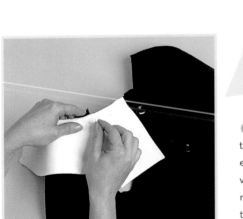

5 Turn the collar right side out, pushing the points out carefully, then press flat. Pin each undercollar to the right side of the waistcoat neck edge, then baste and machine-stitch the neck edge of the collar to the neck edge of the waistcoat. Clip into the seam allowance at regular intervals, then fold it to the inside and baste in place.

method...

6 Work a row of large gathering stitches between the large dot markers on the sleeve cap. Now pin and machine-stitch both sleeve seams with right sides facing, then press the seam open. Fold a 1/2-in. (1.5-cm)-double hem around the lower edge of each sleeve; stitch close to both folded edges forming a casing for the elastic. Thread elastic through the casing.

7 Turn each sleeve right side out but keep the waistcoat wrong side out. Place the sleeve inside the armhole, matching the seam to the notch on the front armhole and the center of the sleeve cap to the notch on the back armhole. Pin in place, then pull up the gathering stitches so the sleeve cap fits neatly. Machine-stitch in place.

8 Make two 12-in. (30-cm)-long ties for a decorative bow at the neckline (*see page 19*). Sew the end of each tie to the front on each side of the top button so the collar will hide the stitching and the raw end of the tie.

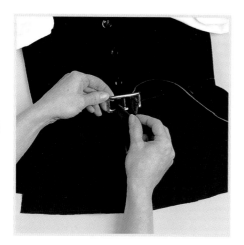

9 Sew the center bar of the silver buckle securely to the center front of the waistcoat at the waistline. Make a narrow belt from the fake leather strip (*see page 19*) to fit the waistline easily; thread it through the buckle. Take the free ends around to the back of the outfit and sew in place at the center back.

FINISHING TOUCHES

Sew on a narrow elastic chin strap when the hat is completed so it stays put when the dog is dressed.

The Hat

1 Make the brim and crown, then attach the crown to the brim by hand as shown (*see pages 20–21*). Make a narrow band from fake leather to match the bodice belt, and thread it through an identical silver buckle. Wrap the band around the hat, then secure in place with a few stitches at the back where the ends overlap.

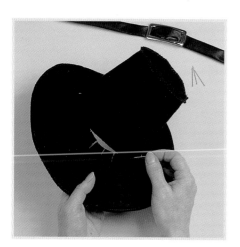

Just promise me this is only for Thanksgiving!

Law and Order

a dog's gotta do what a dog's gotta do...

Apart from the Duke, and Gary Cooper, who does law 'n' order better than your loyal hound? He'd do it even better if he could dress the part. Let him mosey on down to the shindig at the OK Corral fully equipped with ten-gallon hat, a chambray shirt with mighty purty cowboy collar tips, mock suede vest, authentic bandanna, and a shiny sheriff badge (a dog star?). Some law dogs may appreciate a little backup—try a small toy gun belt with plastic pistols; others rely on their canine charisma.

YOU WILL NEED

Basic sewing kit
(*see pages 8–9*)

Dog Smokey. Forget Deputy Dawg—here's a natural-born sheriff

Fake leather strip black, ⁵/8 yd. (50 cm)

5–8 hook-and-loop fastener dots white

5 small shirt buttons (color optional)
2 fake leather buttons for waistcoat

3 decorative conchas
2 collar tips

Sheriff badge
Bandanna
Chin straps

Red felt ⁵/8 yd. (50 cm)
Blue chambray 1¹/8 yd. (1 m)
Mock suede ⁵/8 yd. (50 cm)
Heavyweight iron-on interfacing ¹/2 yd. (50 cm)
Lightweight iron-on interfacing ¹/4 yd. (20 cm)

method...

The Shirt

1️⃣ Trace the patterns given on pages 104–105 to full size, and cut out pattern pieces in fabric and interfacing as directed. Fuse the lightweight interfacing to the wrong side of the two undercollar pieces. Pin the top collars to the undercollars with right sides facing, then stitch together around three sides, leaving the neck edge free. Join the shoulder seams of the shirt bodice with right sides facing, and then press open. Fold and press a 1-in. (2.5-cm) hem down both center back and center front edges. Position hook-and-loop fastener dots on the back opening, as shown, then stitch in place (*see page 18*).

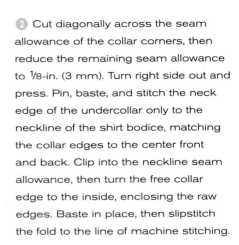

2️⃣ Cut diagonally across the seam allowance of the collar corners, then reduce the remaining seam allowance to 1/8-in. (3 mm). Turn right side out and press. Pin, baste, and stitch the neck edge of the undercollar only to the neckline of the shirt bodice, matching the collar edges to the center front and back. Clip into the neckline seam allowance, then turn the free collar edge to the inside, enclosing the raw edges. Baste in place, then slipstitch the fold to the line of machine stitching.

3 Topstitch the collar and the center front opening in a contrasting thread; we used white, but you could use a brighter color or even a decorative embroidery setting on your sewing machine. Fold and stitch a $3/8$-in. (1-cm) double hem along the lower edges of the shirt. Overlap the center front edges, then sew on several white buttons to secure them; this way, you don't have to make any buttonholes. Attach the collar tips.

Now don't go putting any fancy fringing on that—I sure as heck don't wanna be lookin' sissy in front of the boys!

4 Pin and machine-stitch both sleeve seams with right sides facing; press the seam open. Now turn up and stitch a $3/8$-in. (1-cm) double hem along the lower edge. Turn both sleeves right side out, but keep the shirt wrong side out. Pin the sleeve into the armhole, matching the seam with the notch on the front armhole and the center of the sleeve cap with the notch on the back armhole. Baste and then machine-stitch. Insert the other sleeve in the same way.

method...

The Vest

1 Pin and machine-stitch the vest shoulder seams with right sides facing, then press open. Carefully fold and baste a narrow hem along all the raw edges; machine-stitch. If your fabric is non-fraying, you can just leave the edges unfinished; or trim them neatly with pinking shears if you have these.

FINISHING TOUCHES

Don't forget the elastic chin strap to keep the hat on the dog's head.

2 Fold and press a 1-in. (2.5-cm)-wide hem along both center back edges. Place the loop part of three hook-and-loop fastener dots on the underlap side of the opening and the hook part on the underside of the overlap. Now stitch down the center of the hook-and-loop dots, securing both the hem and the dots at the same time.

The Hat

1 Fuse heavyweight interfacing to one brim piece, then pin the other piece on top, sandwiching the interfacing in between. Join the side of the crown by overlapping the center back edges by 3/8 in. (1 cm) and stitching by hand or machine. Pin the top to the upper edge of the crown, then hand-sew or machine-stitch in place.

2 Machine-stitch close to the outer edge of the brim, and clip into the seam allowance of the inner edge. Bend the resulting tabs so that they lie at right angles to the brim. Place the crown on the brim so the tabs stand up inside the crown. Hand-sew securely in place. Make a narrow mock leather band to fit around the hat, then thread on three decorative conchas. Wrap the band around the hat, and sew them together where they overlap at the back. Sew an elastic chin strap to the inside of the hat.

If the posse heads into town, I'm armed and ready to resist!

Hot Dog

he's just good enough to eat...

Hot dogs, hot dogs—get your hot dogs here! Let's face it, there can be only one costume suitable for the classic sausage dog! Red, here, looks very tasty indeed, nestling comfortably between the two halves of this particularly authentic-looking giant bun. Any hot dog, of course, would be naked without a great big squirt of fake tomato ketchup (or mustard, if you prefer); this one's made from thick fabric-covered batting, with wire in the middle to keep the shape. Standard Dachshunds are all similar in size, but the costume can easily be scaled down to fit the Miniature variety.

YOU WILL NEED

Basic sewing kit
(*see pages 8–9*)

Kitchen knife
large, sharp, with
smooth edge

Spray paints brown,
white or cream, yellow

**Heavy-gauge
galvanized wire**
$1/12$ in. (2 mm)

Dog Red, a cool hot
dog if ever we saw one

Pliers to cut
the galvanized
wire to size

Foam bolster
cylindrical, to shape
the hot dog bun

Thick marker
optional

**Beige
moleskin
fabric** $1^{1}/8$ yd.
(1 m)
Red felt
$3/8$ yd. (30 cm)
Thick batting
$3/8$ yd. (30 cm)
**Hook-and-
loop tape**
$3/8$ yd. (30 cm)

method...

The Bun

1 Trace the patterns given on pages 106–107 to full size, and cut out pattern pieces in fabric as directed. Measure the dog from the neck to the base of the tail. Mark this measurement on the cylindrical foam bolster right around the circumference, using a dark marker pen. Take a large, sharp, smooth-bladed kitchen knife, and cut carefully along the marked line. Use a slow, sawing action to cut though the foam cleanly. You will now need to divide the foam cylinder lengthwise into two equal halves; use the marker pen again to indicate the correct cutting line.

My legs may be little but I've got a HUGE appetite.

2 On the flat underside of each half, use the marker to trace a gently rounded cutting line at both ends. Cut off the corners initially using the kitchen knife. Now turn the foam halves flat side down on your work surface, and snip away slivers of foam, little by little, using large scissors to create a rounded shape at each end. It may take a little time to achieve a smooth, symmetrical shape at both ends.

3 Run a line of large gathering stitches between the large dots on the top bun pieces at both ends. Pin the top bun pieces to the flat bun bases with right sides facing along the straight side edges. Now pull up the gathering stitches so the curved ends match. Pin in place, then stitch together leaving a 12-in. (30-cm) gap in the stitching at the center of one straight side.

4 Turn both fabric bun pieces right side out, then insert a foam shape into each one. You will probably have to squash and wrestle each shape into the fabric cover, since the fit is designed to be snug! Turn in the seam allowance along the opening, and pin the folds together; slipstitch the opening neatly by hand to close. Rearrange the gathers, if necessary, to fit neatly around each curved end.

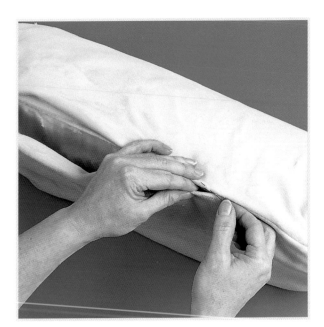

FINISHING TOUCHES

Always use matching thread for slipstitching edges together so the join will be neat and inconspicuous.

method...

5 To make the bun halves look authentic, you'll need to add some color. Spray paint is best for this because the colors will blend smoothly, creating a more realistic appearance. Lay the bun halves on a spare sheet of paper, then spray on a fine layer of brown paint to the main area, applying it more thinly toward the edges. Add a touch of yellow paint toward the edges and, finally, a fine dusting all over with white or cream. You could also spray paint the front chest strap to match your dog's color.

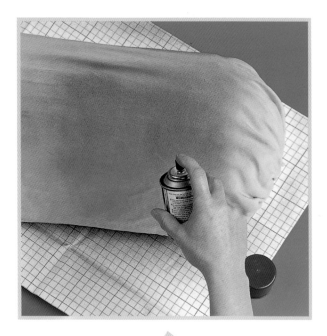

NOTE

Always use spray paints in a well-ventilated area, and remember to wear a mask, too.

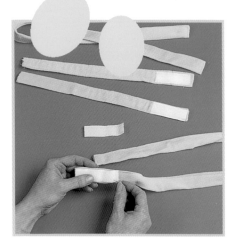

6 Your dog will need a few straps to keep the bun in place—one around the chest, one across the front, and one for the waist. Cut the straps to size (*see pattern pages, 106–107*). For the chest and waist straps, fold and press 3/8 in. (1 cm) across both the short ends and then the same down each side, fold the straps in half lengthwise, then machine-stitch together close to the edges. Now stitch 3-in (8-cm)-long hook-and-loop tape pieces to each end; remember that the loop part needs to be on the underlap and the hook part on the overlap. Make the front chest straps in the same way, but leave one end unfinished. Sew one half of a piece of hook-and-loop tape to the other end.

7 Place the front chest straps in position on the flat side of the bun halves, about halfway down the front edge and 4 in. (10 cm) in from the end. Hand-sew the straps securely, first checking that the straps are positioned so that the hook-and-loop tape pieces will meet and close when the ends are overlapped.

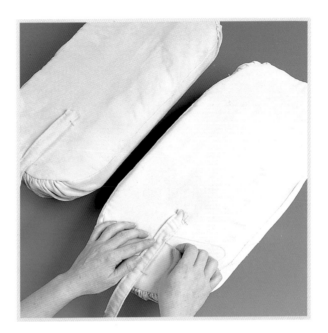

8 Now for the hot dog's chest and waist fastenings. Lay both the straps in the correct position on the flat side of the bun halves; the chest strap should cover the inner end of the front chest strap. Hand-sew both straps securely in place.

Do you think my butt looks big in this?

method...

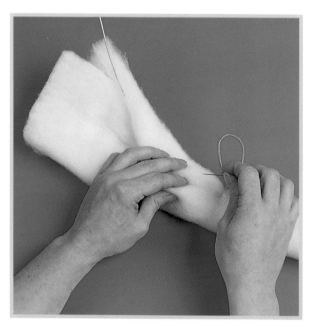

Ketchup

① This is the fun part! A hot dog would be undressed without a suitable accompaniment—ketchup or mustard, as you like. The squirt of ketchup, when straight, should be approximately twice the length of the bun. Cut the fabric to size, then, using pliers or a wire cutter, cut a length of galvanized wire about 2 in. (5 cm) shorter than the fabric piece. Cut a piece of thick batting the same length as the wire and 6 in. (15 cm) wide. Wrap the batting around the wire and sew it in place, as shown.

② Place the roll of batting on the wrong side of the red fabric strip. Wrap one raw edge around the batting, and pin in place. Fold a 3/4-in. (2-cm) hem across the other long edge and press flat using your fingers. Bring the fold up to overlap the first raw edge; pin and hand-sew the fold in place. Tuck in the raw ends and slipstitch them together.

3 The ketchup squirt has to have a nice wavy wiggle. This is easily achieved thanks to the wire inside the padded fabric tube. Just bend the tube into the desired shape—but not too sharply or it will be difficult to straighten out completely if you need to reshape. Try to make soft bends, so the fabric doesn't wrinkle around the corners.

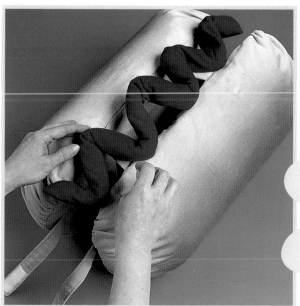

4 Hold the bun steady on your work surface as shown, then lay the ketchup squirt on the straps. Reshape to fit if necessary. When you are satisfied, pin the ketchup to the straps, then sew it securely in place by hand.

Fairy Dog

a magical makeover for any mutt...

They say that beauty is only skin deep—but what a lot of skin! This beautiful wrinkly fairy queen would give any Titania or Tinker Bell a run for her money. Rolie looks extremely pretty in this pink satin dress with glossy ribbon bows decorating the shoulder and waistline, along with a froth of matching pink net to form a cute little tutu. No fairy outfit would be complete without a diamond-encrusted crown and a pair of delicate gossamer wings—purchased from a costume store, of course, unless you really want to work hard. Fancy dress is supposed to be fun, so give yourself a break!

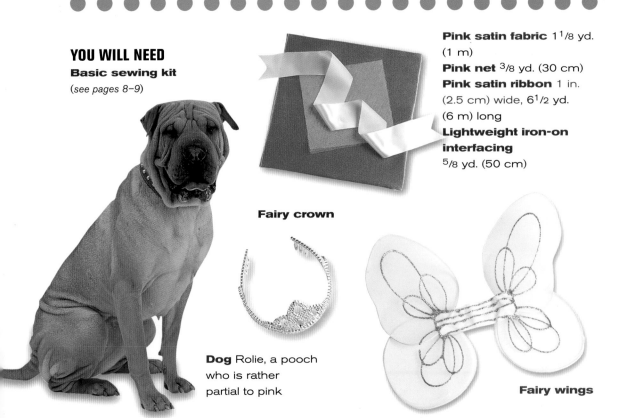

YOU WILL NEED
Basic sewing kit
(see pages 8–9)

Pink satin fabric 1 1/8 yd. (1 m)
Pink net 3/8 yd. (30 cm)
Pink satin ribbon 1 in. (2.5 cm) wide, 6 1/2 yd. (6 m) long
Lightweight iron-on interfacing
5/8 yd. (50 cm)

Fairy crown

Dog Rolie, a pooch who is rather partial to pink

Fairy wings

method...

The Dress

① Trace the patterns given on pages 108–109 to full size, and cut out pattern pieces in fabric and interfacing as directed. Fuse the interfacing to the wrong side of all facings. Pin and machine-stitch the bodice front to the backs, right sides facing, at the side seams only, then press seams open. Join the front facing to the back facings in the same way at the side seam only; press the seams open. Pin the facing to the bodice with right sides together. Fold down the shoulder seam allowance on the facings, as shown, then stitch around the neckline and armholes only. The shoulder seam allowance on the bodice will be free.

FINISHING TOUCHES

To save yourself some work, pop down to your nearest fancy-dress store, and buy a sparkly fairy crown and delicate wings.

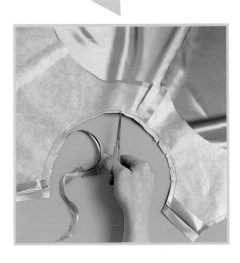

② To reduce bulk, trim the seam allowance around the neckline and armholes to about ⅛ in. (3 mm). Then, using a pair of small, sharp scissors, clip into the raw edges at intervals of about 1 in. (2.5 cm). The clips will allow the curved armhole and neckline to lie smooth and unwrinkled when the bodice is turned right side out.

3 Turn the faced bodice right side out, and press. Now cut four 20-in. (50-cm) lengths of pink satin ribbon, and trim one end of each piece into decorative fishtail points. Place the ribbons together in two pairs, then pin the untrimmed ends to the raw seam allowance at each front shoulder as shown. Baste the ribbons in place to prevent them from sliding out of position.

4 Place the bodice front and back shoulder edges together, enclosing the ribbon ends. Pin and baste, as shown, then machine-stitch, taking care not to catch in the facings as you stitch. This joins the seams and secures the ribbons at the same time.

I want to see quality stitching, lady—we're talking couture here!

method....

5 Open out the shoulder seam and press it flat between your fingers. Tuck the raw ends of the ribbons and the fabric underneath the folded seam allowance facing on each side. You can now slipstitch the seam allowance facing together neatly with matching sewing thread. Finish both shoulders in this way.

6 Open out the facings at center back; turn the seam allowances along the center back edge of each facing to the wrong side; press. Prepare 6 fabric ties (*see page 19*), leaving one end unfinished. Pin them to the center back edges, at waist and neck edges and halfway between. Bring the folded edge of each facing back to the correct position; pin. Stitch ³⁄₈ in. (1 cm) from both center back edges, securing the facing, folds, and ties.

7 For the tutu-style skirt cut a 12-in. (30-cm)-wide strip of pink net, using the whole width of the fabric. For even gathers, divide both the net strip and the waistline edge into quarters and mark with pins. Run a line of machine-gathering stitches across the top of each marked quarter on the net strip. Now pin the net to the waistline with right sides facing, matching up the pin-marked quarters. Gather up the net to fit, then pin and stitch in place.

8 The raw edges of the gathered net are quite scratchy, so bind the seam to prevent irritation to the dog's skin, as follows. From the remaining satin fabric, cut a 2-in. (5-cm)-wide bias strip long enough to fit the waistline seam. Pin and stitch the strip to the waist seam, placing the right side of the strip on the wrong side of the seam, on the net side. Fold in the free edge of the binding, then bring it over the seam allowance to enclose all the raw fabric edges. Slipstitch the fold to the original stitching line. Tuck in the ends of the binding at the center back neatly, and slipstitch to finish.

Some day my Prince will come. . .

9 Cut 4 24-in. (60-cm) lengths of ribbon; trim the ends into fishtail points. Fold ribbons in half lengthwise, and crease sharply to mark the center. Sew the center point of each ribbon to the waistline: two at the front and one on each back piece. Tie waistline and shoulder ribbons into bows. Slip the dog's front legs through the elastic loops on the wings. Attach the crown with the attached combs, or sew on a chin strap.

Dino Dog

give me a home where the dinosaurs roam...

A simple all-in-one Jurassic disguise for Spice the Greyhound. Very happily retired now, Spice was once a professional racing dog and quite accustomed to wearing a coat, but not quite like this! There's a line of magnificent spiky fins, or plates, along the spine and even a tail with pointed arrowhead at the end. As an added bonus, there's no complicated fitting required—simply extend the legs and lengthen or shorten the body part of the pattern to fit potentially prehistoric pooches of all sizes. Okay, so the original stegosaurus wasn't red with green spots, but there's nothing wrong with a bit of artistic license, is there?

YOU WILL NEED

Basic sewing kit
(*see pages 8–9*)

Hook-and-loop tape black, 4 in. (10 cm)

Craft adhesive extra-sticky

Toothpicks

Narrow elastic black, 24 in. (60 cm)

Dog Spice, a chilled-out dog who likes to get a little spiky now and again

Red moleskin fabric 1⁵/8 yd. (1.5 m)
Green felt ⁵/8 yd. (50 cm)
Heavyweight iron-on interfacing 1/4 yd. (20 cm)

method...

Finned Outfit

1 Trace the patterns given on pages 110–111 to full size, and cut out pattern pieces in fabric and interfacing as directed. Fold the seam allowance along the sloping edge of both tail pieces to the wrong side, then pin and machine-stitch. Lay one half of the main body flat on your work surface. Pin the base of the tail to the top rear end of the body, straight tail edge upward and right sides facing, as shown. Machine-stitch in place, then join the other tail and body pieces in the same way.

Underneath this placid exterior is a ferocious stegosaurus just itching to get out!

2 Fuse heavyweight interfacing to half the fin pieces, then place them together in pairs with the unstiffened pieces, enclosing the interfacing. Using red thread, topstitch all the fins close to the curved edge, then stitch a narrow, pointed channel up the center of each fin to hold the toothpicks. Make sure that all the lines of stitching stop about 1 in. (2.5 cm) short of the lower straight edge. Break each toothpick to the correct length for each fin, then slide them carefully into the stitched channels, as shown.

③ Lay one half of the dino body flat on your work surface, then pin the fins along the center back edge, as shown, matching the flat lower edge of each fin with the upper edge of the back. Place the larger fins in the middle of the back and the smaller ones along the upper tail and neck. Place the other body piece on top, right sides facing, enclosing the fins; pin, baste, and stitch the center back and tail seam.

④ For the fins to stand up independently, the seam allowance at the lower edge of each must be opened up and topstitched securely. On the wrong side, flatten out the seam allowance of each fin and baste it in place, as shown. From the right side, topstitch about ¼ in. (6 mm) away from the fin down each side of the seam.

⑤ Fold and baste a narrow hem along all the remaining raw edges of the body and feet; take care that the fabric does not wrinkle too much when going around the curved edges. Machine-stitch, using matching sewing thread, then press the edges so they lie flat.

method...

⑥ Glue the large and small colored felt spots in a random pattern to the main body of the dino costume on both sides, then glue three claws to each foot. Use quick-drying extra-sticky craft glue for this.

⑦ Pin a foot piece to the end of each leg, so that the curved edge of the leg covers the raw top edge of the foot. Pin or baste in place, then stitch securely by machine or hand.

⑧ The costume has two shaped tabs at the front chest, which form an overlapped fastening. Cut a 2-in. (5-cm) piece of hook-and-loop tape, and sew the loop part to the underlap and the hook part to the overlap.

9 To keep the legs in position and to prevent the feet flapping around, attach a 6-in. (15-cm) piece of elastic to the wrong side of the leg where the feet are stitched on. Secure the ends using double thread and several backstitches. The headdress (*see* Finishing Touches *below*) can be held to the dog's head in the same way with an elastic chin strap.

FINISHING TOUCHES

Make a little headdress complete with fins to match the outfit (template on page 110). Construct in the same way as the main garment.

10 To complete the costume stitch the green arrowhead shape to the end of the tail with contrasting red topstitching. Finally, hand-sew a few snap fasteners to the wrong side of the tail's hemmed edge so it will fit snugly around the dog's tail.

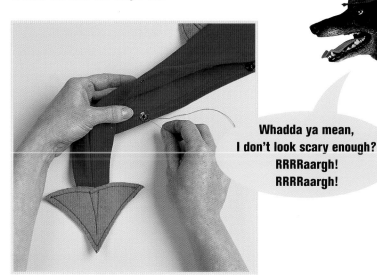

Whadda ya mean, I don't look scary enough? RRRRaargh! RRRRaargh!

Prince of Darkness

Bela Lugosi, eat your heart out...

Dracula must be one of the all-time fancy-dress favorites. This classic costume is instantly recognizable—simple yet stylish. Crisp white shirt front, neat bow tie, then the trademark voluminous black satin cape with a blood-red lining, draped impressively around the shoulders. Halloween can't come soon enough, but remember: partying for this Prince is strictly confined to the hours of darkness—from dusk till dawn only.

● ●

YOU WILL NEED

Basic sewing kit
(*see pages 8–9*)

Hook-and-loop tape
white,
2 in.
(5 cm)

Black satin fabric
1 3/8 yd. (1.2 m), 48 in.
(120 cm) wide

Red satin fabric
1 3/8 yd. (1.2 m), 48 in.
(120 cm) wide

White cotton fabric
3/8 yd. (30 cm)

Lightweight iron-on interfacing
3/8 yd. (30 cm)

Dog Huxley, a dog that sleeps by day and bites by night

4 small white buttons

Decorative cord fastener black

method...

Dracula's Shirt

 Trace the patterns given on pages 112–113 to full size, and cut out pattern pieces in fabric and interfacing as directed. First, fuse the lightweight interfacing to the wrong side of both shirt fronts, two tie pieces, and two undercollars. Now fold and press a 1-in. (2.5-cm) hem down the center front of each shirt piece, then fold and stitch a narrow single hem along the curved outer edges and across the shoulder. Pin the tie and the collar pieces together with right sides facing; machine-stitch. Trim across the seam allowance at collar points, as shown, then reduce the seam allowances along stitched edges on both collar and tie.

 Turn the two collars and ties right side out, and press, making sure that all the points are neatly pushed through. Pin the right side of the interfaced undercollar to the right side of the neckline, as shown, matching the center fronts of the collar and the shirt. Machine-stitch, then reduce the seam allowance to about ¼ in. (6 mm) and clip the curved edge in a few places.

3 Fold the raw seam allowances along the neck edge of the top collar and undercollar to the inside and press flat with your fingers. Bring the folded edge of the top collar toward the neckline, enclosing all the raw edges; baste in place. Slipstitch the fold to the line of machine stitching. To finish the back collar, continue slipstitching the folded edges together neatly. Cut a 1-in. (2.5-cm) piece of hook-and-loop tape, then sew the loop part to the underlap of the back collar and the hook part to the overlap.

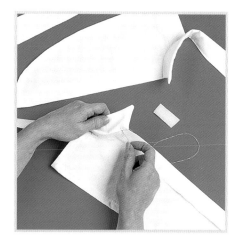

I'm a fiendish hound, but I'll sit up and beg . . . for blood!

4 Hand-sew the narrow ends of each bow tie piece to the front neckline, just below the collar. Make two 20-in. (50-cm) long ties from white fabric (*see page 19*); stitch to each side of the shirt front as shown—you could use white ribbon for this as an alternative. Tie in a bow around the Prince's waist to keep the shirt front in place. Overlap the center fronts by 1 in. (2.5 cm), then sew on four small white buttons to secure.

method...

Dracula's Cape

1 Pin and baste the cape and lining together, with right sides facing, around the outer curved edge and the two straight front edges, as shown, leaving the curved neckline free; machine-stitch. Trim diagonally across the corners at the lower front edge and reduce all other seam allowances. Clip the seam allowance at intervals along the outer curve. Turn the cape right side out, and press.

2 Fuse lightweight interfacing to the wrong side of the undercollar, then pin it to the top collar with right sides facing. Machine-stitch together, leaving the neck edges free. Trim diagonally across the seam allowance at the corners, and reduce the seam allowance to ¼ in. (6 mm). Turn the collar right side out, and press.

3 Pin and stitch the right side of the interfaced undercollar to the right side of the cape neckline, matching the center front edges of cape and collar. Fold the seam allowance of the top collar neck edge to the inside, and press it flat with your fingers. Reduce the seam allowance to about 1/4 in. (6 mm), and clip at intervals. Bring the folded edge to meet the neckline, enclosing all the raw edges. Now slipstitch the fold to the line of machine stitching.

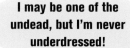

I may be one of the undead, but I'm never underdressed!

4 To complete the cape, carefully hand-sew a decorative black cord fastening to the center front, using black thread. Position the two halves of the fastener just below the collar, making sure that the cord loop and button will meet neatly. (Hold the fastener in place with a few small spots of glue while you stitch, because it would be difficult to pin.)

Coco the Clown

send in the dogs...

Step right up, folks! Come and see this delightful duo of dotty Dalmatians, Disney and Domino, looking absolutely fabulous in their Coco the Clown costumes. It would be a shame to hide their gorgeous spotted coats, so we chose simply to accessorize them with brightly colored ruffles and headgear. The leg and neck ruffles are identical for each outfit, but there's a choice of two classic hats, Pierrot and Jester, for variety. For that special finishing touch, add some jingly bells and fluffy pompoms—just make sure that they're firmly stitched and glued on. Barnum and Bailey would have been proud.

YOU WILL NEED

Basic sewing kit
(see pages 8–9)

Dogs Disney and Domino, who just love clownin' around

Yellow cotton fabric
3/8 yd. (30 cm), 43 in. (110 cm) wide
Red cotton fabric
3/8 yd. (30 cm), 43 in. (110 cm) wide
Medium-weight iron-on interfacing
1/4 yd. (20 cm)

Rickrack
yellow, 3 3/8 yd. (3 m)

Narrow elastic
white, 1 3/8 yd. (1.2 m)
Craft adhesive
extra-sticky and quick-drying

5 small bells

Ribbons red and yellow satin

Pompoms
red and yellow

Red felt
5/8 yd. (50 cm)
Yellow felt
5/8 yd. (50 cm)

method...

Leg Ruffles

1 Trace the patterns given on pages 114–115 to full size, and cut out pattern pieces in fabric and interfacing as directed. For each leg ruffle you'll need one strip in each color. Pin the strips together with right sides facing, then machine-stitch together down each long side, leaving the short ends free. Turn right side out, and press. Now, using small running stitches, join the short ends of the red (or yellow) sides, as shown, with right sides facing, leaving the other side open.

2 Thread a 10-in. (25-cm) piece of narrow elastic through the leg ruffle, using a large safety pin attached to one end. When the elastic has been passed throughout the ruffle, tie the ends together in a secure knot, then turn in the unstitched edges and slipstitch them together neatly.

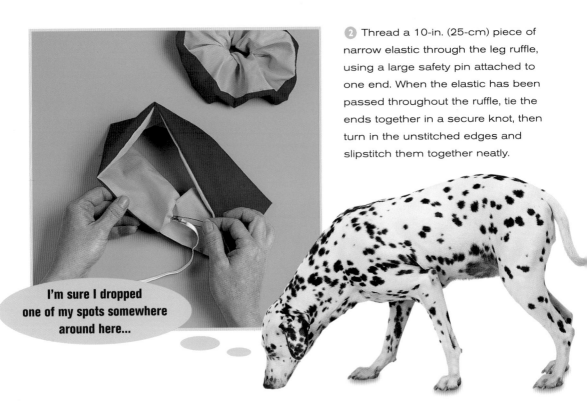

I'm sure I dropped one of my spots somewhere around here...

Neck Ruffle

1 You will need one of the larger strips in each color for the neck ruffle. Pin the strips together around all four sides with right sides facing; stitch, leaving a gap in the stitching of about 2 in. (5 cm) at one short end. Trim diagonally across the seam allowance at each corner, then turn the strip right side out, and press.

2 Make a casing for the ribbon ties across one long side of the ruffle by machine stitching about 1/2 in. (1.5 cm) from one long edge. Unpick the seam at each end of the casing to enable the ribbon to be threaded through. Now pin and stitch a length of decorative rickrack braid to the lower edge of the ruffle; you can glue this in place if you're in a hurry.

3 Thread a length of satin ribbon through the casing at the neck edge of the ruffle, using a large safety pin attached to the end. Gather up the ruffle until it matches the dog's neck measurement. Machine-stitch across both ends of the casing, securing the ribbon. Leave about 12 in. (30 cm) of ribbon free for ties, then trim the ends into neat fishtail points.

method...

Clown Hats

① For the Jester hat front and back, pin and stitch one red and one yellow piece together as shown, taking a 1/4-in. (6-mm) seam allowance only. For the Pierrot hat, pin and stitch one red and one yellow piece together along the straight edges, again taking only 1/4-in. (6-mm) seam allowance and leaving the lower curved edges free.

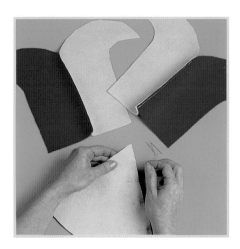

② Stitch the front and back of the Jester hat together with right sides facing. Turn both hats right side out. Fuse medium-weight interfacing to all brim pieces of both hats. Join the brims together in pairs at the center front: overlap the edges by 1/4 in. (6 mm), then stitch from the right side. For each hat, both brim pieces should have the same color on the right when right side up.

③ Place the brim pieces together with the wrong sides facing and topstitch close to the curved outer edge. Now tuck the inner edge of the brim under the lower edge of the hat as shown, and overlap by 1/4 in. (6 mm); pin in place, then overlap the short ends of the brim at the center back. Stitch the brim overlap together, then stitch the brim to the hat from the right side. Attach the brim to the other hat in the same way.

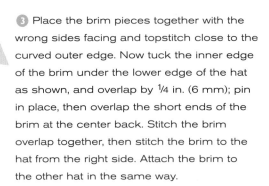

FINISHING TOUCHES

Hand-sew an elastic strap to each hat to keep it in place on the dog's head when he's wearing it.

④ To complete the Jester hat, sew a small brass bell to the end of each point, then glue a large pompom to the center front— use quick-drying, extra-sticky craft glue. To make sure the hats keep their shape, stuff the points with lightweight tissue paper.

⑤ Glue some decorative fluffy pompoms in graduated sizes to the front of the cone-shaped hat, then sew short lengths of red and yellow ribbon to the tip. Trim the ends of each ribbon to neat fishtail points, then sew a small brass bell to each.

"Tears of a clown?" I'm having the time of my life!

Blues Brothers

every doggy needs somebody!

They're called Eggs and Chips and they're on a mission from God! They've got sharp suits, white shirts, black ties, porkpie hats, and they've even got the cool wraparound shades just to prove that they mean business! This sharp-suited canine look can be adapted for other well-known screen characters, too. How about a smooth-talking (or smooth-barking) agent 007 James Bond, for example, or a couple of "Men in Black?" Alternatively, you can use the costume (minus the porkpie hat and the shades of course) for a simple classic black-tie look for a formal social occasion.

YOU WILL NEED

For each costume
Basic sewing kit
(*see pages 8–9*)

Dogs Eggs and Chips—a cool canine combination

Black felt fabric
5/8 yd. (50 cm)
White cotton fabric
1/4 yd. (20 cm)

Hook-and-loop tape black, 1/4 yd.– 5/8 yd. (20–50 cm)
Hook-and-loop tape white, 2 in. (5 cm)
Lightweight interfacing
1/4 yd. (20 cm)

Narrow elastic black, 3/8 yd. (30 cm)
Fake leather strip black, 5/8 yd. (50 cm)
3 small black buttons

Cool shades

method...

I'm expecting nothing less than Savile Row quality!

Jackets

1 Trace the patterns given on pages 116–117 to full size, and cut out pattern pieces in fabric and interfacing as directed. Fold both the collar pieces in half with wrong sides facing and notches matching; the felt is quite firm and does not require interfacing. Stitch across both short ends of each collar close to the edge. Now pin the front and back jacket pieces together at the shoulders, with right sides facing. Machine-stitch, taking a $1/2$-in. (1.5-cm) seam allowance, and press the seam open.

2 Pin the prepared collars to the right side of the jacket matching the leading wider edge of the collar with the notch on the neckline, which indicates the center front, and the narrower collar edge with the center back. Baste in place, then machine-stitch through both layers of the collar. Pin and stitch the front facing to the jacket with right sides together along the center front edge and around the neckline to the shoulder. The facing is just long enough to meet the shoulder seam.

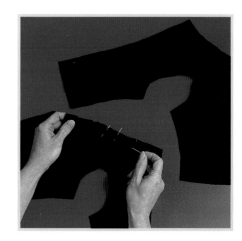

❸ Trim diagonally across the seam allowance of the corner at the front neck edge, then clip into the curved neck edge several times so the seam will lie flat. Turn the facing to the wrong side, making sure that the point is pushed out neatly, then press. Baste through all layers close to the neckline seam and then down the front edge, in preparation for topstitching. Cut a length of hook-and-loop tape to fit the center back opening. Sew the loop part to the underlap and the hook part to the overlap of the opening.

❹ Pin and stitch the side edges together with right sides facing, then press the seam open. Fold and stitch a $^3/8$-in. (1-cm) single hem at the lower edge of both sleeves, then join the sleeve seam with right sides facing. Turn each sleeve right side out. If the costume is a bigger size, the sleeve hem can be stitched after the sleeve seam has been joined.

❺ Turn both sleeves right side out, but keep the jackets wrong side out. Place the sleeve in the armhole, matching the seam with the notch on the front armhole and the center of the sleeve cap with the notch on the back armhole. Pin in place, baste, and stitch. Insert the other sleeve in the same way.

method...

6 Turn the jacket right side out, then topstitch the front edges and collar with matching sewing thread. Overlap the center front edges of the jacket by about 1 in. (2.5 cm), then sew on three small black buttons as decoration and to secure the opening.

Hats

1 Overlap the short edges of the crown side by ¼ in. (6 mm), pin, and hand-sew them together. Pin the top to the side, baste, and hand-sew with tiny stitches, taking ¼ in. (6 mm) seam allowance. Turn crown right side out. Overlap the short edges of the brim by ¼ in. (6 mm), pin, and sew by hand.

FINISHING TOUCHES

Make a narrow band from a strip of fake leather and sew it around each hat, overlapping the ends at the center back.

2 Pin the brim to the crown, wrong sides facing, aligning the overlapped (center back) seams; baste, as shown, then sew them together securely by hand. If the hat is a large size, this might be done by machine.

Shirts and Ties

1 Fuse lightweight interfacing to the wrong side of the undercollar half of each collar piece. Fold the collar in half with right sides facing, then stitch across the two shorter ends, leaving the neck edge free. Turn the collar right side out; press. Turn in the seam allowances along the neck edge, and slipstitch the folded edges together; press.

2 Overlap the collars at the center front by about 3/8 in. (1 cm), and secure them with a few hand stitches in matching thread. Cut a 1-in. (2.5-cm) length of hook-and-loop tape; sew the loop part to the underlap side at the collar back and the hook part to the overlap.

Hey, which one of you wiseguys just called us a couple of cool CATS?

3 Make a tie from a folded fake leather band (*see page 19*). Cut off a short 2-in. (5-cm) length, then wrap this around the end of the remaining strip to suggest a knot. Trim the end of the tie into a point, then sew the knot to the front of the collar.

Space Dog

to boldly go where no dog has gone before...

Houston... we have a problem—there's a dog in space! Before your astro-pooch goes rocketing into orbit at warp factor 10, make sure that he's fully equipped with this stunning silver spacesuit and padded metallic vest. Little Charlie's space pants even have a gap in the back seam so that he can happily waggle his little tail unhindered. This space dog's crowning glory has to be the papier-mâché helmet. Not all dogs will be happy to wear one, but Charlie loved it—well, that is until he decided it was much better as a soccer ball. One small step for a dog, one giant leap for canine kind.

YOU WILL NEED

Basic sewing kit
(*see pages 8–9*)

Face mask
Marker pen

Silver satin fabric
$1^1/8$ yd. (1 m)
Silver quilted fabric
$5/8$ yd. (50 cm)
Elastic white, $1^5/8$ yd.
(1.5 m)

Newspaper
Wallpaper paste
Bowl
X-Acto knife
Paintbrush

Hook-and-loop tape
white, 2 in.
(5 cm)
Spray paint
silver

Masking tape
Balloon
1 snap fastener
Sandpaper

Dog Charlie; his ambition is to be the first (and best-dressed) dog on Mars

method...

Space Helmet

① In a bowl, mix up a small quantity of wallpaper paste as directed on the package. Inflate a balloon to the size required for the dog's head, then, using tabs of masking tape, attach it to a large cup or bowl for stability. Tear some sheets of newspaper into strips about 1-in. (2.5-cm) wide and coat with wallpaper paste using a paintbrush. Lay the pasted strips smoothly on the balloon. Build up about three overlapping layers in this way, then allow to dry.

② When the papier-mâché is completely dry, remove the tabs of masking tape, and pop the balloon to release the shape. Mark the neck edge and face area using a dark marker. Using sharp scissors, trim along the neck edge, then cut out the face area, using an X-Acto knife. If necessary, use a piece of sandpaper to smooth out any roughness along the cut edge.

③ Mark a hole about 3/8 in. (1 cm) in diameter at the center back of the helmet about 1 in. (2.5 cm) up from the neck edge. Cut out carefully, using an X-Acto knife. When the dog is dressed up, you can thread the ties at the back of the spacesuit top through this hole, then tie in a bow to attach the helmet to the suit during "flight."

4 Place the space helmet on a large piece of paper, and apply two or three even layers of metallic silver spray paint, allowing each layer to dry before applying the next. Always use spray paint in a well-ventilated area, and remember to wear a face mask. Apply paint to the inside of the helmet in the same way.

How many ears does a Space Dog have? Three! The right ear, the left ear, and space, the final frontier!

Spacesuit Top

1 Trace the patterns on pages 118–119 to full size, and cut out in fabric. Pin and machine-stitch both sleeve seams with right sides facing; fold and stitch a 1/2-in. (1.5-cm) double hem at the lower edge of each sleeve. Pin and stitch the shoulder seams with right sides facing; fold and stitch a narrow double hem down both center back edges. Press the hems flat and the shoulder seam open. Turn sleeves right side out, but keep the bodice inside out. Place the sleeve in the armhole, matching the seam with the notch on the front armhole and the center of the sleeve cap with the notch on the back armhole. Pin, then machine-stitch. Insert the other sleeve in the same way.

method...

2 Take the precut bias strip that will form the neck binding and ties, and pin it to the neckline with right sides facing. Match the center of the binding with the center front neck, so that there will be an equal amount on both sides at the back for the ties. Machine-stitch the binding to the neckline, then clip into the seam allowance at 1-in. (2.5-cm) intervals so that the binding will lie smooth when complete.

3 Fold the remaining long raw edge toward the center of the binding, and pin. Fold and pin about 1 in. (2.5 cm) in at both short ends. Now fold the parts of the binding that form the ties in half to enclose all the raw edges, then bring the folded edge around the neck to meet the stitching line. Pin and then slipstitch the folded edges of the ties together; similarly, slipstitch the binding to the stitching at the neckline.

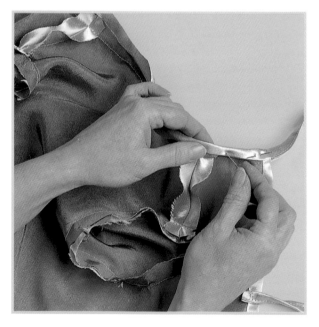

Spacesuit Pants

1 First pin and stitch the inside leg seams of the pants with right sides facing, then join the crotch seam, leaving a small gap in the stitching between the dots, for the tail. Fold and pin a ½-in. (1.5-cm) double hem at the waistline edge to make a casing for the elastic. Do this on the waistline edge of the spacesuit top, also. Machine-stitch close to the fold of each casing and close to the garment edge. Finally, fold and stitch a narrow double hem at the ankle edge of the pants. Press all seams open and hems flat.

NOTE
This plasticized metallic-finish fabric requires a nonstick Teflon-coated machine foot to aid smooth topstitching.

2 Cut two lengths of thin elastic, long enough to stretch around the dog's waist quite snugly, but not too tight, then allow about 4 in. (10 cm) extra for the knot. Unpick a few stitches of the center back seam between the casing stitching lines at the center back of the pants to enable the elastic to be threaded through. Now pass the elastic through the casings on the pants and top, using a large safety pin attached to the end. Knot the ends of the elastic together securely.

method...

Padded Space Vest

① Pin and stitch the center back seam with right sides facing, from the lower edge up to the marked dot. This creates a small opening at the back neck, which allows the dog's head to pass through easily. Pin and stitch both shoulder seams together with right sides facing.

To infinity and beyond!

② Fold and baste a narrow single hem around the neckline and the lower and side edges, then machine-stitch. Remember to use a nonstick Teflon-coated machine foot for this, or the fabric may drag under the foot.

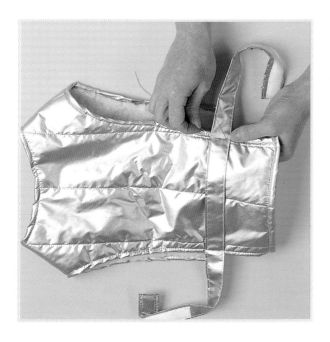

③ Cut the belt piece from the padded fabric, then discard the batting and use the thin shiny top layer only. Press a narrow hem along both short ends and then down each long side. Fold the strip in half lengthwise, then stitch together close to the folded edge and across each end. Cut 2 3-in. (8-cm) pieces of hook-and-loop tape, then sew the hook part only to the underside of each end of the belt. Try the vest on the dog to find a suitable position for the belt. Remove the vest, pin the belt in place on the front, then hand-sew it securely to the hemmed side edges as shown.

④ Cut 2 1-in. (2.5-cm) pieces from the leftover loop half of hook-and-loop tape, and sew it to the back of the vest in a suitable position corresponding to the hook part on the belt. For the neck tab, cut a 1-in. (2.5-cm) x 2-in. (5-cm) rectangle from a scrap of metallic fabric. Fold a narrow single hem across the short edges, then down each long side, then fold the tab in half, bringing the short edges together. Machine-stitch close to the edge on all four sides. Stitch the tab to one side of the back neck opening, then sew the ball part of a snap fastener to the underside. Sew the other half of the snap to the other side of the opening.

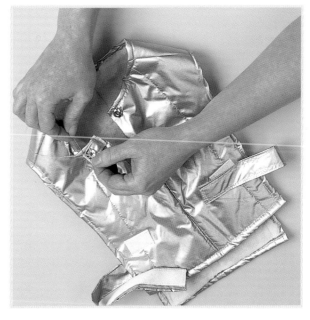

Doctors and Nurses

your life in their paws...

Or should I say Dog-tor and Nurse? These costumes definitely come as a pair—Dr. Kildare ready to go into the O.R. in surgeon's scrubs and Nurse Betty in classic uniform with crisp white apron and cap. When you're creating costumes for your doggy friends, add good accessories for that professional finishing touch. A quick search in a local thrift shop resulted in a real stethoscope and fob watch for next to nothing—perfect.

YOU WILL NEED

Basic sewing kit
(*see pages 8–9*)

Dogs Yogi and Towser, famed for their smooth bedside manner

Stethoscope
Fob watch
Eyeglasses light, plastic (optional)

2 soft cleaning cloths
Narrow elastic white, 1 1/8 yd. (1 m)

Hook-and-loop fastener white, 6 1/2–12 1/2 in. (17–32 cm)

Green cotton fabric
1 5/8 yd. (1.5 m)
Blue and white striped cotton fabric
1 1/8 yd. (1 m)
White cotton fabric
3/8 yd. (30 cm)
Lightweight iron-on interfacing
1/8 yd. (20 cm)

method...

Doctor's Outfit

①　Trace the patterns on pages 120–121 to full size, and cut out pieces in fabric and interfacing as directed. Fuse lightweight interfacing to the wrong side of the front and back facings. Pin and stitch the shoulder seams of the facings and the doctor's gown together with right sides facing. Press all seams open. Lay the facing on the gown neckline with right sides together. Pin, baste, and stitch the facing to the neckline, matching the shoulder seams and the V at the center front. At the point of the V, clip into the seam allowance up to the stitching line, taking care not to cut the stitches. Reduce the seam allowance to about ¼ in. (6 mm), then fold the facing to the inside of the gown.

Keep your paws to yourself, Nurse Betty, I've got doggy lives to save!

②　Press the neckline seam flat, then baste through the gown and facing to hold the layers in place. Using matching sewing thread, topstitch the neckline from the right side, about 1 in. (2.5 cm) away from the edge. This has a decorative purpose and acts to keep the facing flat. Join both sleeve seams with right sides facing, then press open. Now fold and stitch a ½-in. (1.5-cm) double hem along the lower sleeve edges. Turn both sleeves right side out, but keep the gown wrong side out. Place the sleeve in the armhole, matching the seam with the notch on the front armhole and the center of the sleeve cap with the notch on the back armhole. Pin, baste, and machine-stitch. Insert the other sleeve in the same way.

3 Fold and machine-stitch a ¹/2-in. (1.5-cm) double hem down both back edges and along the lower edge of the gown, then press. Make 6 12-in. (30-cm)-long ties (*see page 19*) and pin them in place along each side of the back opening at the neck edge, the middle of the back, and waist level, as shown. Secure the end of each tie with a few hand stitches.

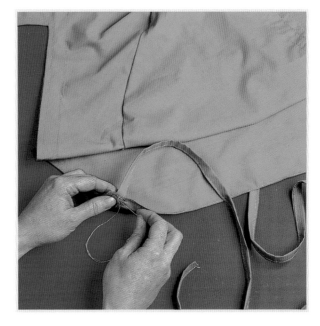

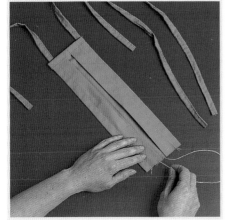

4 Fold and press a narrow double hem along both long edges of the mask, then fold and press an inverted pleat at the center; baste it in place, as shown. Fold a small double hem at both short edges, then machine-stitch. Prepare 4 ties, then sew one to each corner of the mask by hand (far end of the mask is shown finished). Your dog will not like to wear the mask on his face, so just tie it around his neck.

Optional Hat

1 Pin and stitch the two semicircular hat pieces together, leaving two gaps in the stitching for the ears. Fold and stitch a ¹/2-in. (1.5-cm)-wide single hem around the circumference of the circle. Unpick a few stitches in the hem as shown to allow the elastic to be threaded through. Attach a large safety pin to the end of the elastic, then pass it through the casing. Gather up the elastic to fit snugly around the dog's head, then tie the ends together in a knot.

method...

Nurse's Outfit

1 Fuse lightweight interfacing to the undercollar section, then pin and baste the two collar sections together, right sides facing. Machine-stitch, leaving the neck edge free. Trim the seam allowance, and trim diagonally across the corners at the center front and back. Press a 1-in. (2.5-cm) hem down both center back edges of the bodice, then stitch the loop parts of three hook-and-loop dot fasteners to the underlap and the hook parts to the overlap. Pin the shoulder seams together with right sides facing; machine-stitch.

2 Run a line of gathering stitches on each sleeve cap (*see page 15*). Join both sleeve seams with right sides facing, then fold and stitch a 1/2-in. (1.5-cm) casing on the lower edges. Thread with elastic, and knot the ends securely. Turn the collar right side out, and press. Pin the interfaced undercollar to the bodice neckline, with right sides facing, edges matching, center front of collar at center front of neck, and ends of collar at center back edges. Baste, machine-stitch, then trim the seam allowances, and clip into the raw edges. Turn under the raw edge of the top collar, and bring the fold to match the line of stitching. Pin, baste, and slipstitch the fold in place.

3 Turn each sleeve right side out, keeping the bodice wrong side out. Place the sleeve cap inside the armhole, matching the seam to the front armhole notch and the center of the sleeve cap to the back armhole notch. Pin, pull up the gathering stitches, and machine-stitch in place. Stitch a narrow double hem at the lower edge of the skirt and on three sides of the apron and bib. Pin apron and bib in place on the skirt and bodice front. Gather up the skirt to fit the waistline; pin, baste, and stitch in place. Turn under and machine-stitch a narrow hem on the side edges of the skirt. Make ties (*see page 19*); sew to waistline at center back.

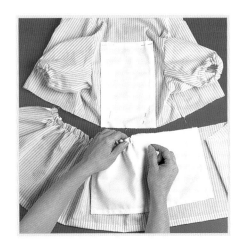

Nurse's Hat

1 Fold hat in half, right sides facing, with shaped edges matching. Stitch long edges together. Turn hat right side out; press flat. Fold hat in half lengthwise; pin the short, center back, edges together, as shown, and stitch.

George Clooney won't be able to resist me in this!

2 Open up the hat and fold it flat so the center back seam lies in the middle. Pin the remaining short ends together, as shown, and machine-stitch. Turn the hat right side out, and fold back the brim. Sew on an elastic chin strap to keep it in place.

Rock 'n' Roll Hero

wild thing, you make my heart sing...

Mr. Jeffries certainly looks like he's lived life in the fast lane, and he's got the longest ears in the business, too—this dog was just born to be wild. Any self-respecting rock 'n' roller would consider himself (or herself—same outfit for the rock chick, too) improperly dressed without the signature leather jacket, bandanna, and classic white T-shirt. The jacket has been tailor-made to fit the doggy physique, but other elements of the outfit can be borrowed from your own closet. Simply use the bandanna as it is, and take the T-shirt in a little at the sides for a snug figure-hugging rock-star silhouette.

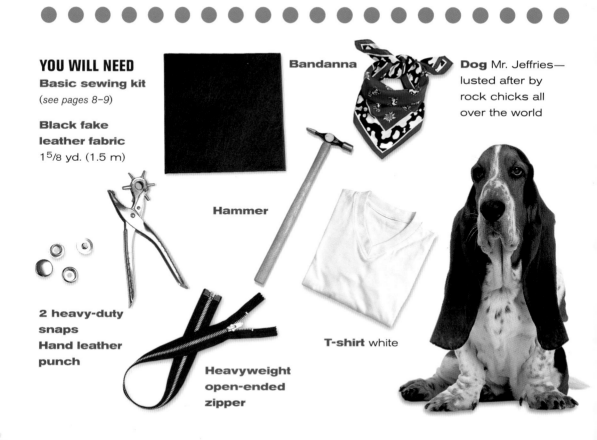

YOU WILL NEED

Basic sewing kit
(*see pages 8–9*)

Black fake leather fabric
1⁵/8 yd. (1.5 m)

2 heavy-duty snaps
Hand leather punch

Hammer

Heavyweight open-ended zipper

Bandanna

T-shirt white

Dog Mr. Jeffries—lusted after by rock chicks all over the world

method...

This jacket had better be ready in time for the next gig.

Jacket

1 Trace patterns given on pages 122–123 to full size, and cut out pattern pieces in fabric as directed. Pin and stitch a center back to a side back with right sides facing, then topstitch the seam from the right side. To do this press both seam allowances in the same direction on the wrong side, then machine-stitch about $3/8$ in. (1 cm) away from the seam from the right side. Pin the yoke to the back, right sides facing, as shown, machine-stitch the seam, then topstitch from the right side.

2 Separate the two zipper halves. Pin the half without the slider, face down, to the long edge of the right side front, with the tape matching the fabric edge; baste in place. Lay the right front on top, with right sides facing; pin and baste. Using the zipper foot, stitch the two sections together, as close as possible to the zipper teeth. On the right side, turn the teeth toward the center, and topstitch through all layers $3/8$ in. (1 cm) from the seam. Now pin the other half, face down, to the long edge of the left front, as shown, and baste in place.

3 Because the fake leather fabric is quite firm, it does not need to be interfaced. Fold both collars in half with right sides facing, then pin and machine-stitch across the short ends, as shown. Cut across the seam allowance at the pointed front corner, then turn both collars right side out. Topstitch about $3/8$ in. (1 cm) from the side and top edges, using matching thread.

4 Lay a back jacket piece on each front piece with the right sides together. Pin the shoulder edges together, as shown; machine-stitch. Press the seam lightly on the wrong side using an iron on a cool setting, but do not open out the seam allowance; make sure that both allowances are folded toward the back. Now turn the jacket right side up, and topstitch $3/8$ in. (1 cm) away from the seam with matching thread.

NOTE
This fake leather fabric requires a nonstick Teflon-coated presser foot to aid free and smooth stitching.

method...

5 Pin the prepared collar to the right front/back neckline, as shown, matching the front edge of the collar with the center front notch on the neckline and the back of the collar with the center back edge. Position the other collar in exactly the same way on the left front/back neckline.

FINISHING TOUCHES

Dress your Rock Dog in a classic white T-shirt—a child's size or an adult's shirt cut down a little. Finally, add a colorful bandanna.

6 Pin the right front facing to the right front underlap, as shown, with right sides facing and front and neck edges matching. Baste and stitch. Apply the other facing to the left front overlap edge in the same way.

7 Trim diagonally across the seam allowance at each top corner, then reduce the remaining seam allowances to about ¼ in. (6 mm). Clip the curved neck seam allowance at intervals of about 1 in. (2.5 cm) so the facing will lie flat. Turn the facing to the underside, then pin or baste near the front edge and around the neckline seam in preparation for topstitching. Topstitch with matching thread about ⅜ in. (1 cm) in from the center front edges and then along the collar and neckline seam.

8 Join both sleeve seams with right sides facing, then press open. Now fold and stitch a ½-in. (1.5-cm) single hem along the lower edge. Pin and machine-stitch the side seams with right sides facing. Press the seam allowance toward the back, using a cool iron, then turn right side out. Topstitch each side seam from the right side using matching thread.

How many times do I have to tell you? My contract explicitly states no ORANGE dog biscuits!

method...

9 Turn both sleeves right side out, but leave the jacket wrong side out. Place the sleeve in the armhole, matching the seam with the notch on the front armhole and the center sleeve cap with the notch on the back armhole. Pin in place and then machine-stitch. Insert the other sleeve in the same way.

10 Cut a length of hook-and-loop tape a little shorter than the center back edge. Pin and machine-stitch the loop part to the underlap side and the hook part to the overlap side, as shown.

11 Pin each waistband to a lower edge, with right side of band to wrong side of jacket, positioning the right band so that only ½ in. (1.5 cm) extends at the front, with the remainder at the back, as shown; reverse this on the left section, so that the band will extend more on the front edge. These extensions are underlaps. Turn back the short seam allowances—not the underlaps; stitch waistbands in place. Turn band to right side, pin over seam as shown, and topstitch.

⑫ Mark the desired position of the snaps on the overlap tab and underlap of the band with a ballpoint pen, then make a hole through the fabric, using a hand leather punch. The punch has a rotating wheel to adjust the size of hole; choose one that is most similar to the diameter of the snap post.

What a stud! I'll be fighting off the chicks now.

⑬ Following the instructions on the package, insert the snaps into the prepunched holes. Usually, the upper and lower part of the snap comes in two parts, which must be hammered together, using the tool provided. The socket part of the snap should be attached to the underlap.

Templates

On the following pages you will find patterns for all the costumes. They can be scaled up to fit any size dog, from a Chihuahua to a St. Bernard. Just follow the simple instructions below.

CANINE VITAL STATISTICS

Measure your dog as shown. When you have worked out his or her size, you can scale the templates up to fit. Each square on the page represents 1 square on your chosen grid.

A Tip of tail to base

B Base of tail to neck

C Paw to hip back leg

D Back leg girth

E Center body girth

F Upper body girth

G Paw to hip front leg

H Front leg girth

I Circumference of head

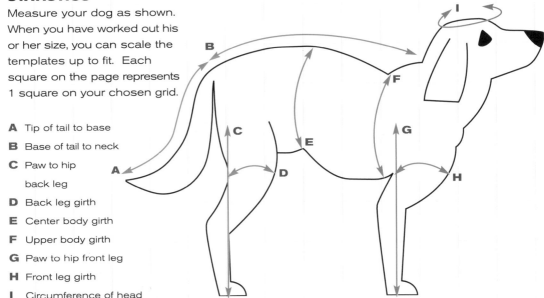

Determining grid and fabric size

To determine which size grid will give you a garment of a suitable size, use the chest size guide to find out whether the dog is small, medium-size, or large:

Small dog: under 20 in. (50 cm) chest

Medium dog: between 20 in. (50 cm) and 28 in. (70 cm) chest

Large dog: between 28 in. (70 cm) and 36 in. (90 cm) chest

Next, using a marker, darken the appropriate lines on the 1-in. (2.5-cm) pattern paper to make a grid of suitable size:

Small dog size . . . . use 1 1/2 in. (3.5 cm) squares

Medium dog size . . use 2 in. (5 cm) squares

Large dog size . . . . use 2 1/2 in. (6.5 cm) squares

Copy the templates onto the enlarged grid (see page 8), and cut out the patterns. Lay the templates on a flat surface covering the width of your chosen fabric (or half the width where pieces are to be cut twice or on a fold), and measure the length covered to determine the amount of fabric required.

Key to symbols

———— Cutting line
– – – – Fold line
– · – · – · – Center line
o—o Straight of grain
•◦◦◦◦◦◦• Gather between dots
Notch for sleeve center, or on armhole
• Stitch to dot
◦◦ Place on fold

Elvis

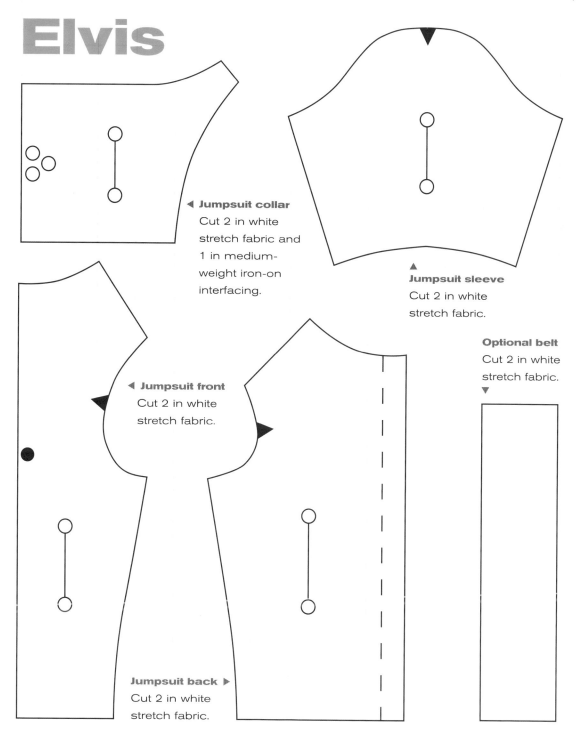

◄ Jumpsuit collar
Cut 2 in white
stretch fabric and
1 in medium-
weight iron-on
interfacing.

▲
Jumpsuit sleeve
Cut 2 in white
stretch fabric.

Optional belt
Cut 2 in white
stretch fabric.
▼

◄ Jumpsuit front
Cut 2 in white
stretch fabric.

Jumpsuit back ▶
Cut 2 in white
stretch fabric.

Pilgrim Father

**Waistcoat
front/back**
Cut 2 in black felt.
▼

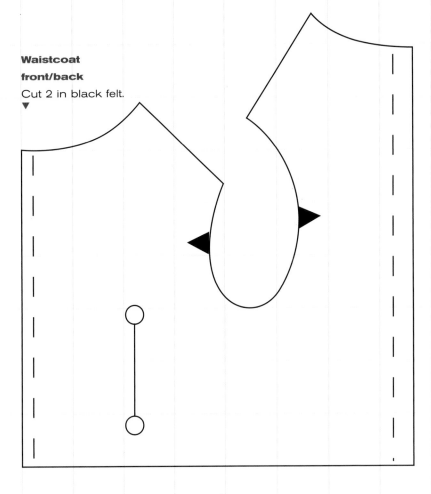

▲
Shirt ties
Cut 2 in white
cotton fabric.

Shirt collar ▶
Cut 4 in white
cotton fabric and
2 in lightweight
iron-on
interfacing.

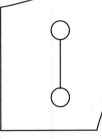

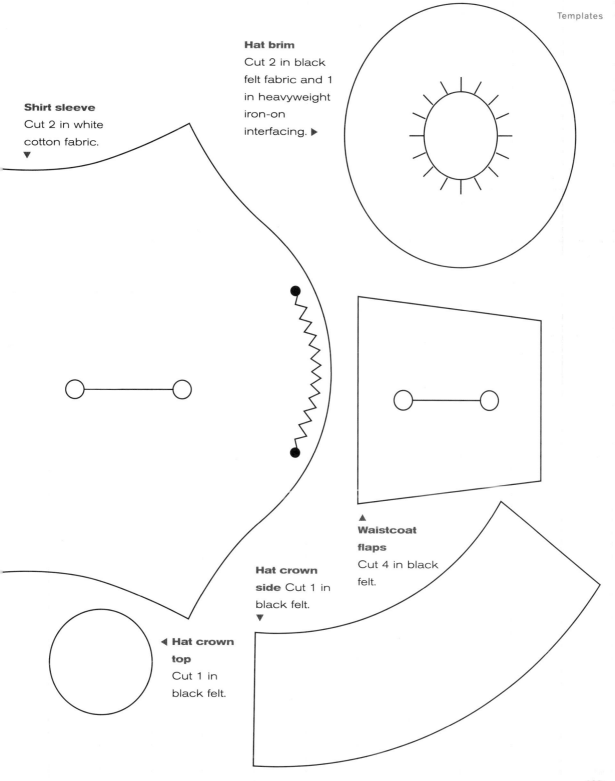

Shirt sleeve
Cut 2 in white
cotton fabric.
▼

Hat brim
Cut 2 in black
felt fabric and 1
in heavyweight
iron-on
interfacing. ▶

▲
**Waistcoat
flaps**
Cut 4 in black
felt.

**Hat crown
side** Cut 1 in
black felt.
▼

◀ **Hat crown
top**
Cut 1 in
black felt.

Law and Order

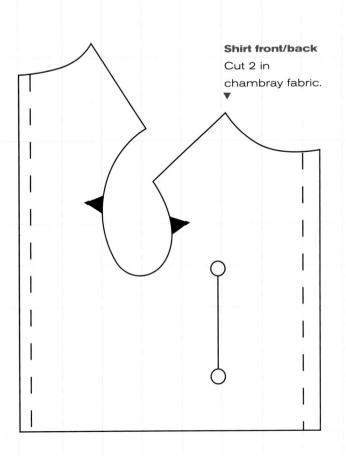

Shirt front/back
Cut 2 in chambray fabric.
▼

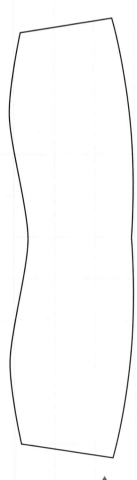

▲
Hat crown, side
Cut 2 in red felt and 1 in heavyweight iron-on interfacing.

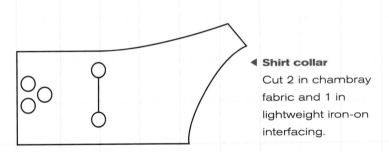

◄ **Shirt collar**
Cut 2 in chambray fabric and 1 in lightweight iron-on interfacing.

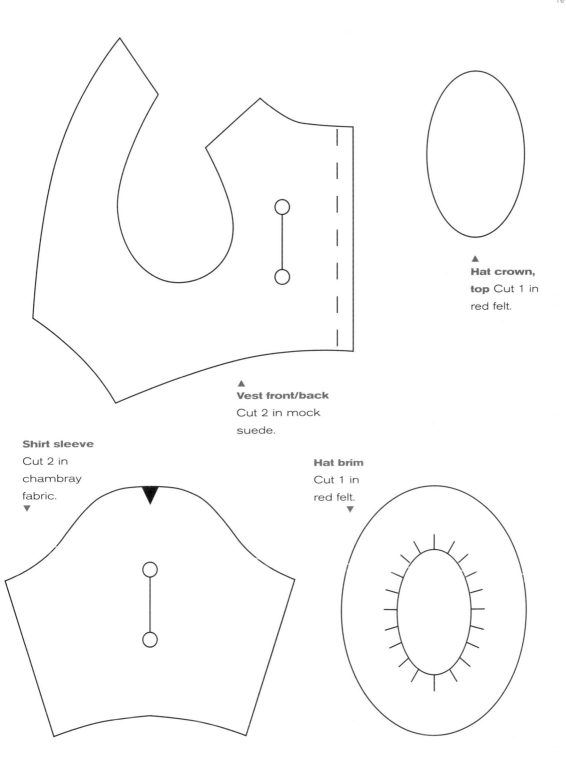

▲
Hat crown, top Cut 1 in red felt.

▲
Vest front/back Cut 2 in mock suede.

Shirt sleeve Cut 2 in chambray fabric.
▼

Hat brim Cut 1 in red felt.
▼

Hot Dog

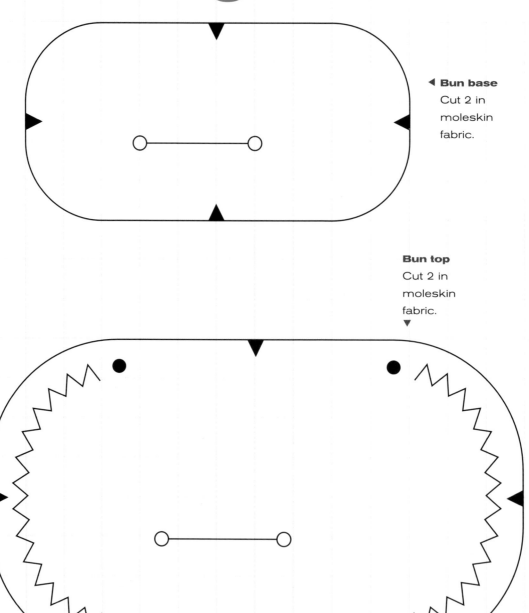

◀ **Bun base**
Cut 2 in
moleskin
fabric.

Bun top
Cut 2 in
moleskin
fabric.
▼

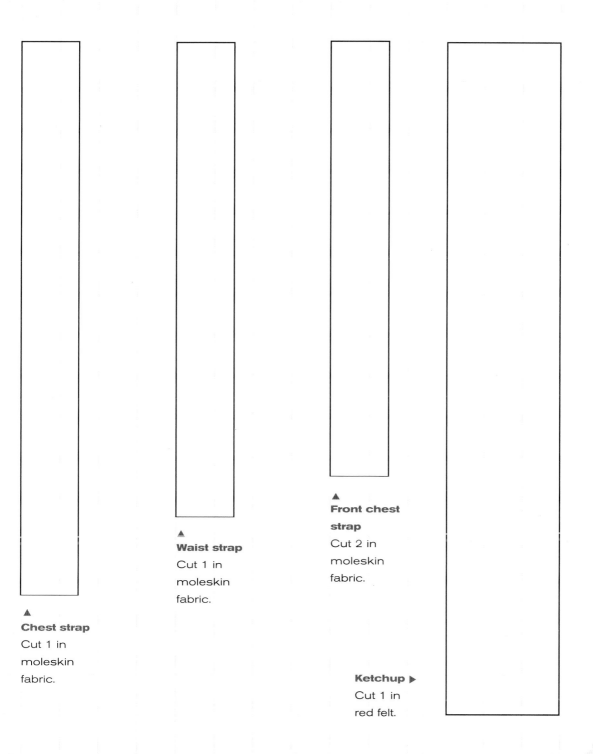

▲
Chest strap
Cut 1 in
moleskin
fabric.

▲
Waist strap
Cut 1 in
moleskin
fabric.

▲
**Front chest
strap**
Cut 2 in
moleskin
fabric.

Ketchup ▶
Cut 1 in
red felt.

Fairy Dog

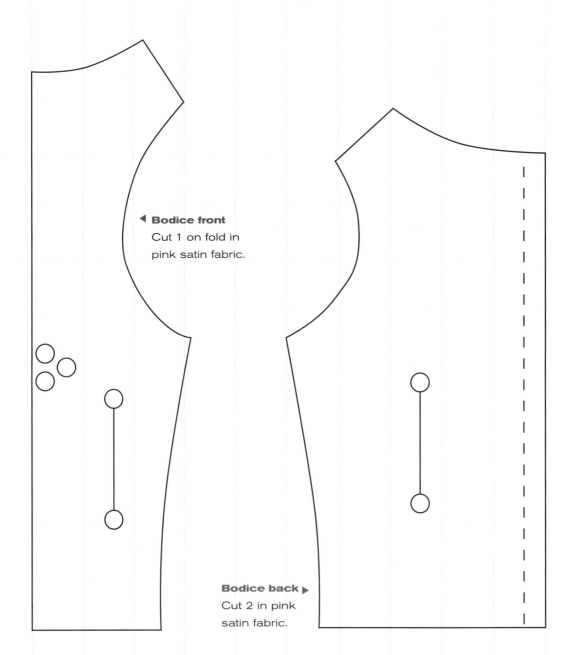

◀ Bodice front
Cut 1 on fold in
pink satin fabric.

Bodice back ▶
Cut 2 in pink
satin fabric.

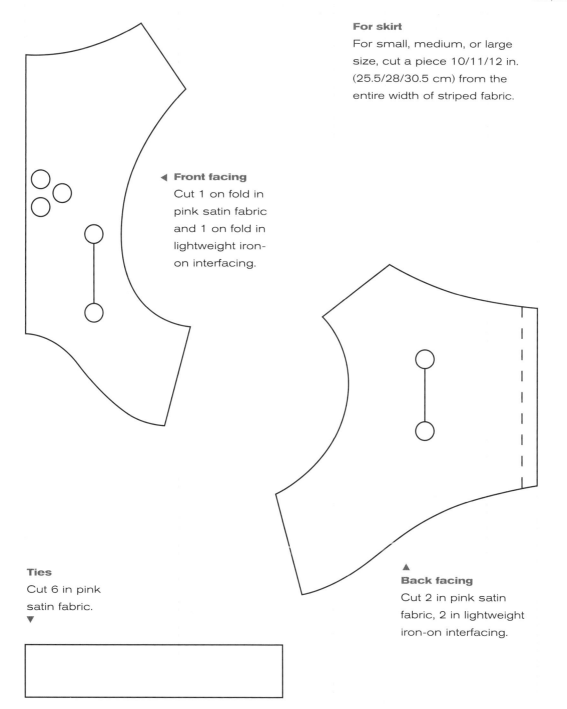

For skirt

For small, medium, or large size, cut a piece 10/11/12 in. (25.5/28/30.5 cm) from the entire width of striped fabric.

◄ **Front facing**
Cut 1 on fold in pink satin fabric and 1 on fold in lightweight iron-on interfacing.

Ties
Cut 6 in pink satin fabric.
▼

▲
Back facing
Cut 2 in pink satin fabric, 2 in lightweight iron-on interfacing.

Dino Dog

Tail arrowhead ▶
Cut 2 in green
felt and 1 in
heavyweight iron-
on interfacing.

▲
Side body
Cut 2 in red
moleskin fabric.

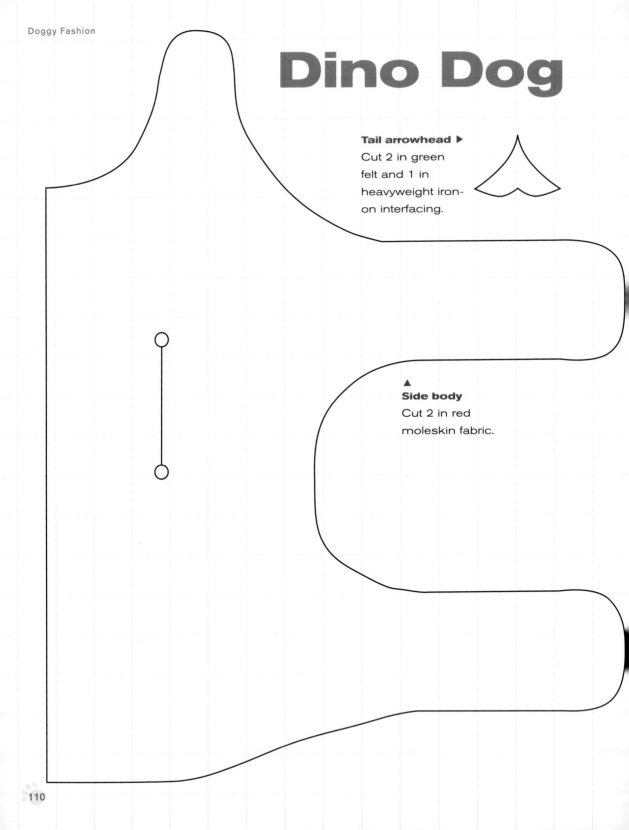

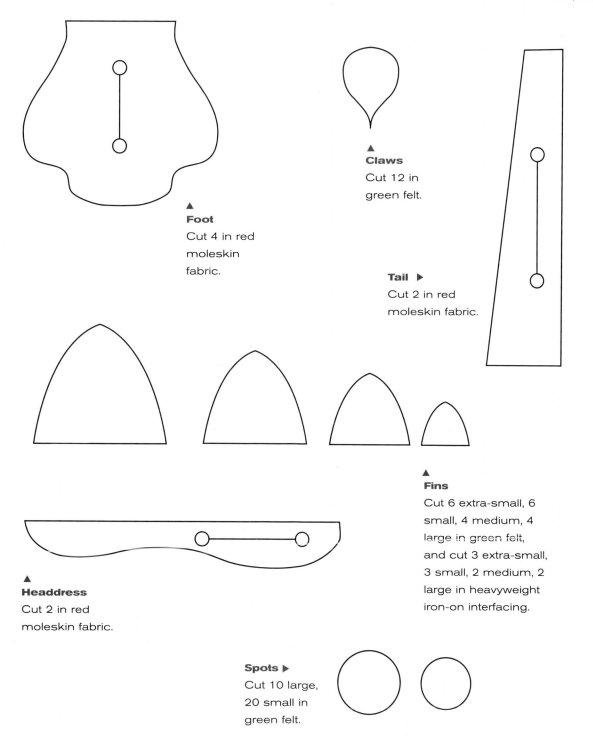

▲
Foot
Cut 4 in red
moleskin
fabric.

▲
Claws
Cut 12 in
green felt.

Tail ▶
Cut 2 in red
moleskin fabric.

▲
Fins
Cut 6 extra-small, 6
small, 4 medium, 4
large in green felt,
and cut 3 extra-small,
3 small, 2 medium, 2
large in heavyweight
iron-on interfacing.

▲
Headdress
Cut 2 in red
moleskin fabric.

Spots ▶
Cut 10 large,
20 small in
green felt.

Prince of Darkness

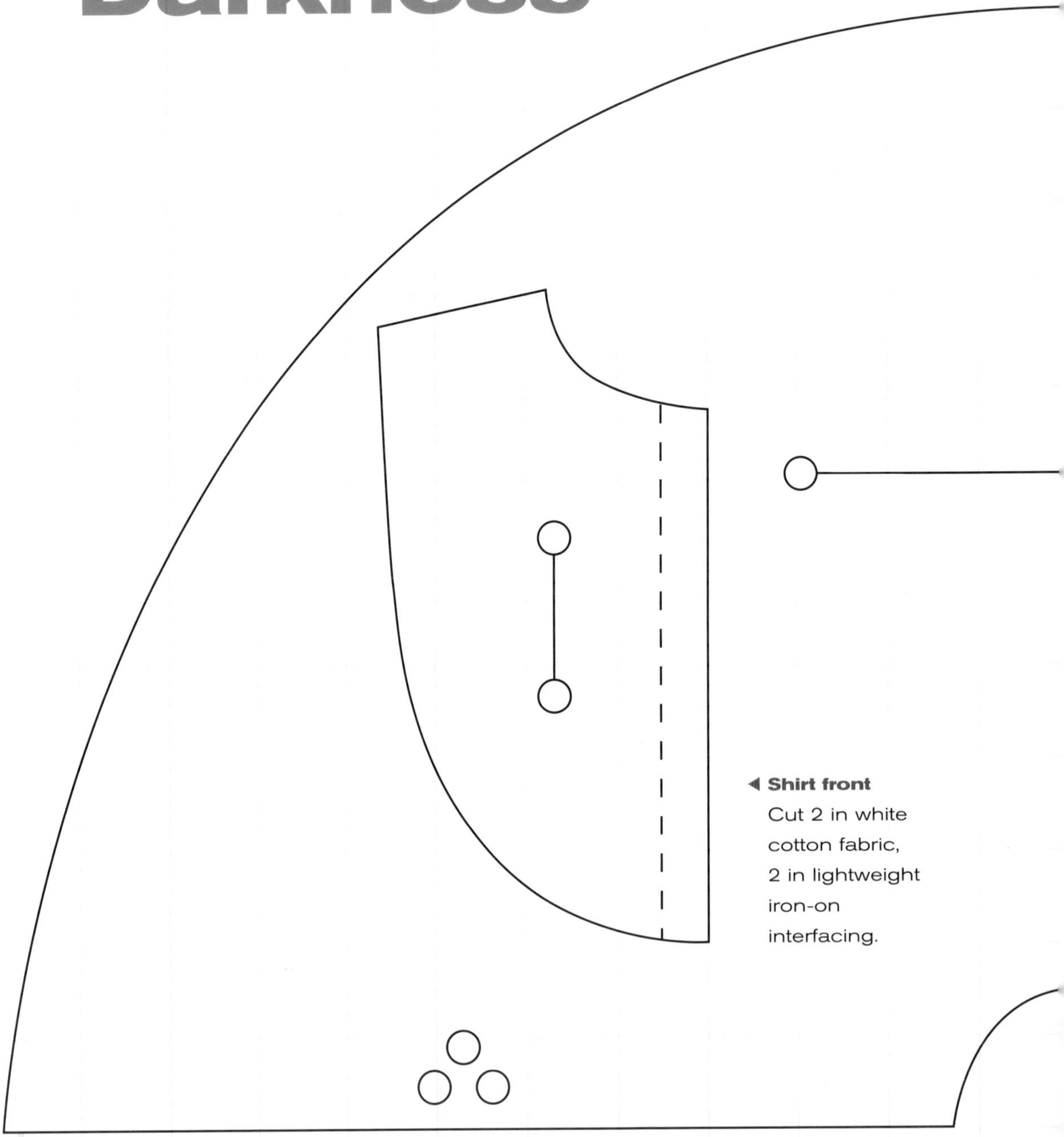

◄ **Shirt front**
Cut 2 in white
cotton fabric,
2 in lightweight
iron-on
interfacing.

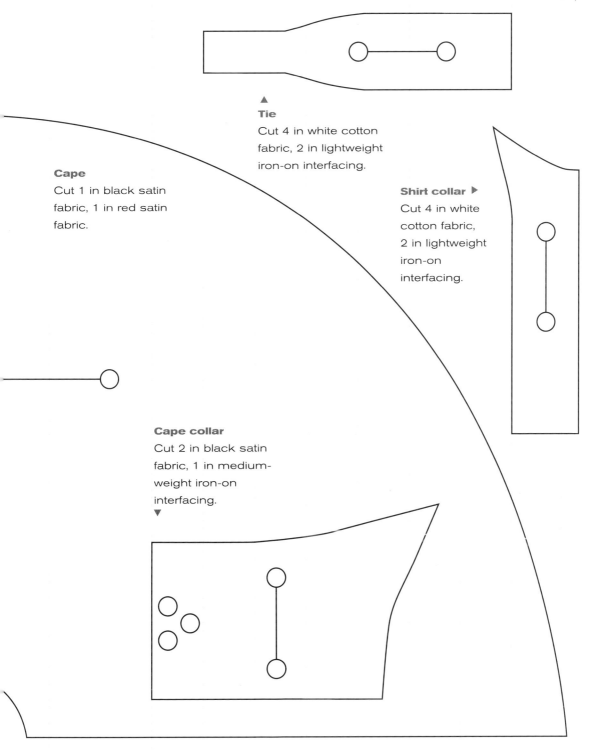

Tie
Cut 4 in white cotton
fabric, 2 in lightweight
iron-on interfacing.

Cape
Cut 1 in black satin
fabric, 1 in red satin
fabric.

Shirt collar ▶
Cut 4 in white
cotton fabric,
2 in lightweight
iron-on
interfacing.

Cape collar
Cut 2 in black satin
fabric, 1 in medium-
weight iron-on
interfacing.
▼

Coco the Clown

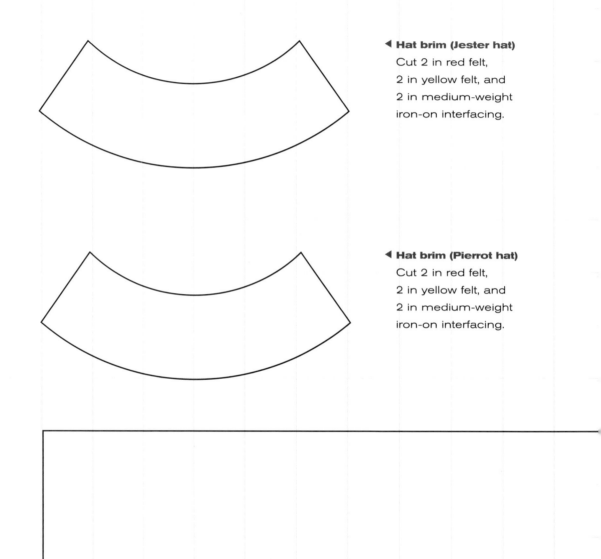

◀ Hat brim (Jester hat)
Cut 2 in red felt,
2 in yellow felt, and
2 in medium-weight
iron-on interfacing.

◀ Hat brim (Pierrot hat)
Cut 2 in red felt,
2 in yellow felt, and
2 in medium-weight
iron-on interfacing.

Pierrot hat ▶
Cut 1 in red,
1 in yellow felt.

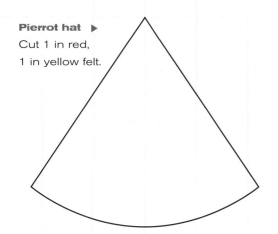

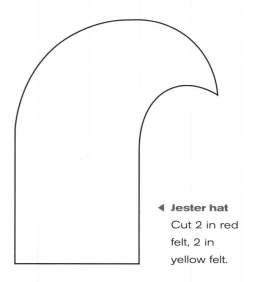

◀ **Jester hat**
Cut 2 in red
felt, 2 in
yellow felt.

Leg ruffles
Cut 4 strips in red
cotton fabric, 4 in
yellow cotton fabric.

Neck ruffle
Cut 1 strip in red
cotton fabric, 1 in
yellow cotton fabric.

Blues Brothers

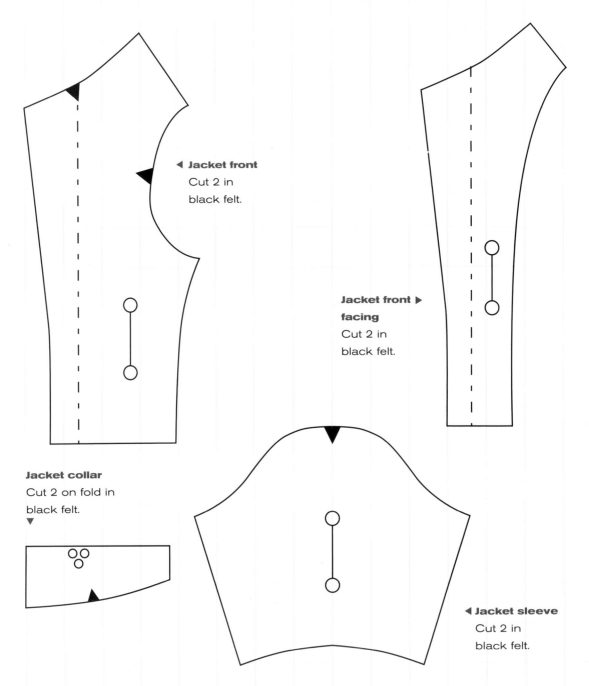

◀ **Jacket front**
Cut 2 in
black felt.

Jacket front ▶
facing
Cut 2 in
black felt.

Jacket collar
Cut 2 on fold in
black felt.
▼

◀ **Jacket sleeve**
Cut 2 in
black felt.

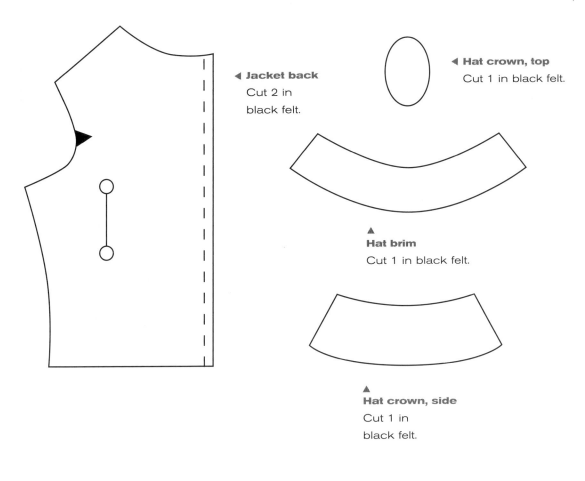

◀ **Jacket back**
Cut 2 in
black felt.

◀ **Hat crown, top**
Cut 1 in black felt.

▲
Hat brim
Cut 1 in black felt.

▲
Hat crown, side
Cut 1 in
black felt.

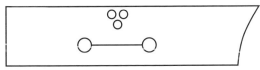

▲
Shirt collar
Cut 2 on fold in white
cotton fabric, 1 in
lightweight iron-on
interfacing.

▲
**Decorative
hat band**
Cut 1 in fake
leather.

Space Dog

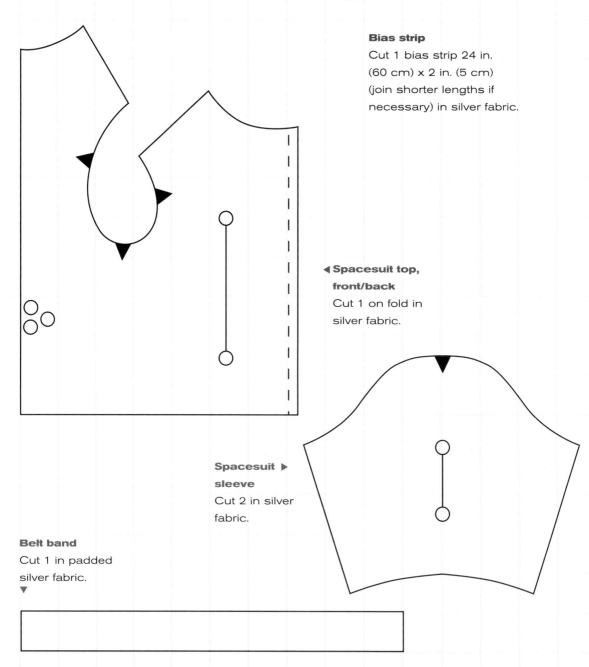

Bias strip

Cut 1 bias strip 24 in. (60 cm) x 2 in. (5 cm) (join shorter lengths if necessary) in silver fabric.

◀ **Spacesuit top, front/back**

Cut 1 on fold in silver fabric.

Spacesuit ▶ sleeve

Cut 2 in silver fabric.

Belt band

Cut 1 in padded silver fabric.

▼

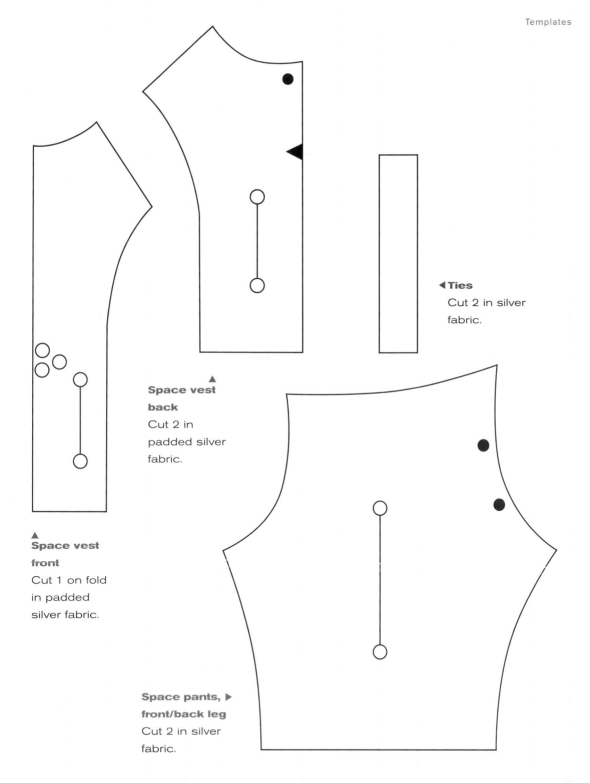

◄ Ties
Cut 2 in silver
fabric.

▲
Space vest
back
Cut 2 in
padded silver
fabric.

▲
Space vest
front
Cut 1 on fold
in padded
silver fabric.

Space pants, ▶
front/back leg
Cut 2 in silver
fabric.

Doctors and...

For gown ties

Cut 6 strips, 12 in. (30 cm) by 2 in. (5 cm) in green fabric.

Gown front/back

Cut 1 on fold in green cotton fabric.

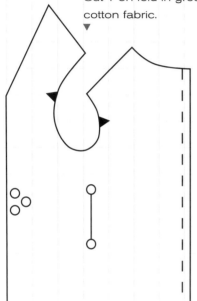

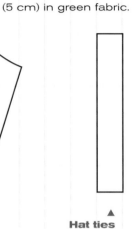

Gown sleeve

Cut 2 in green cotton fabric.

Hat ties

Cut 6 in green cotton fabric.

◄ **Hat**

Cut 2 in cleaning cloth fabric.

◄ **Gown front facing**

Cut 1 on fold in green cotton fabric and 1 on fold in lightweight iron-on interfacing.

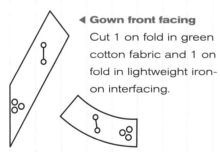

Gown back facing

Cut 1 on fold in green cotton fabric and 1 on fold in lightweight iron-on interfacing.

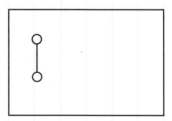

Mask

Cut 1 in green cotton fabric.

Mask ties

Cut 4 in green cotton fabric.

...Nurses

Dress bodice front
Cut 1 on fold in striped cotton fabric.

For dress skirt
For small, medium, or large size, cut a piece 10/11/12 in. (25.5/28/30.5 cm) from the entire width of striped fabric.

◀ Dress bodice back
Cut 2 in striped cotton fabric.

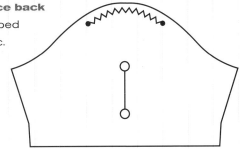

▲ Dress sleeve
Cut 2 in striped cotton fabric.

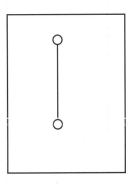

Collar
Cut 2 on fold in white cotton fabric and 1 in lightweight iron-on interfacing.
▼

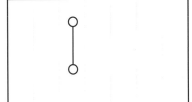

▲ Apron
Cut 1 in white cotton fabric and 1 in lightweight iron-on interfacing.

▲ Apron bib
Cut 1 in white cotton fabric.

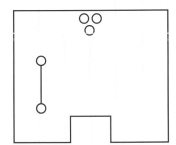

▲ Hat
Cut 1 on fold in white cotton fabric.

Ties
Cut 2 in white cotton fabric.
▼

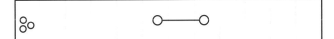

Rock 'n' Roll Hero

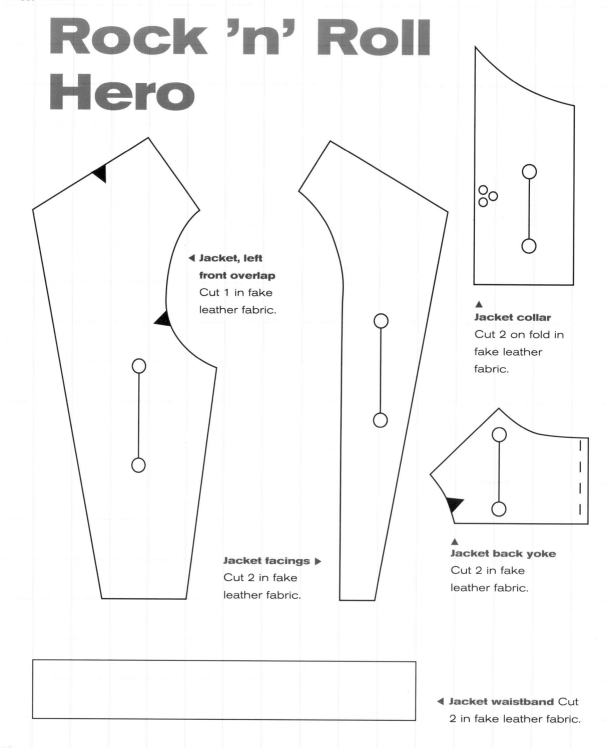

◀ **Jacket, left front overlap** Cut 1 in fake leather fabric.

▲ **Jacket collar** Cut 2 on fold in fake leather fabric.

Jacket facings ▶ Cut 2 in fake leather fabric.

▲ **Jacket back yoke** Cut 2 in fake leather fabric.

◀ **Jacket waistband** Cut 2 in fake leather fabric.

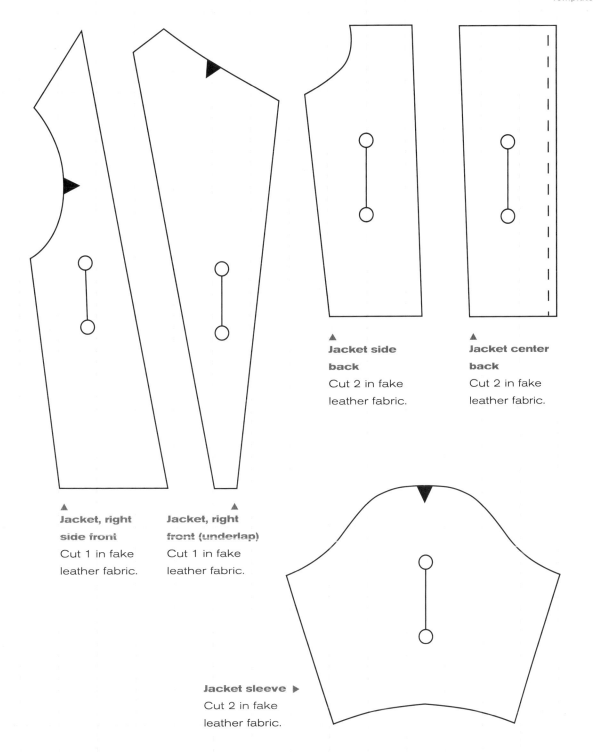

▲
**Jacket side
back**
Cut 2 in fake
leather fabric.

▲
**Jacket center
back**
Cut 2 in fake
leather fabric.

▲
**Jacket, right
side front**
Cut 1 in fake
leather fabric.

▲
**Jacket, right
front (underlap)**
Cut 1 in fake
leather fabric.

Jacket sleeve ▶
Cut 2 in fake
leather fabric.

Resources

Beacon Fabric & Notions
6801 Gulfport Boulevard, South, Suite 10
South Pasadena, FL 33707
Phone: (800) 713-8157 (Toll Free Voice)
Fax: (800) 707-3765 (Toll Free Fax)
www.beaconfabric.com

Clotilde
P.O. Box 7500
Big Sandy, TX 75755-7500
Phone: 1-800-545-4002
www.clotilde.com

The Cottage Discount Needlework
P. O. Box 864691
Plano, TX 75023
Phone: 1-888-227-9988
Fax: (509) 463-3066
www.discountneedlework.com

Crafts Etc!
7717 S.W. 44th Street
Oklahoma City, OK 73179
Phone: 1-800-888-0321 or (405) 745-1200
Fax : (405) 745-1225
www.craftsetc.com

CreateForLess
6932 S.W. Macadam Avenue
Suite A
Portland OR 97219
Phone: 1-866-333-4463
www.createforless.com

Fabrics-Store.com
6325 Santa Monica Boulevard, #102
Hollywood, CA 90038
Phone: (323) 465-8050
Fax: (323) 465-8004
www.fabrics-store.com

Hobby Lobby
6235 North Davis Highway
Pensacola, FL 32504
Phone: (850) 478-4200
www.hobbylobby.com

Joann.com
900 Elmwood Drive
Lansing, MI 48917-2070,
Phone: (517) 323-7660
www.joann.com

Needle In A Haystack
1340 Park Street
Alameda CA 94501
Phone: 877-HAYSTACK (877-429-7822) Toll-free
or (510) 522-0404
Fax: (510) 522-3692
www.needlestack.com

Sewing in the USA
Internet Sales USA
2825 Business Center Boulevard, Suite C-4
Melbourne, FL 32940.
Phone: 1-888-872-7397
Fax: 1-321-254-8477
www.sewinginusa.com

Uncommon Thread, Inc.
Box 338, South Sharon Amity Road
Charlotte, NC 28211
Phone: 1-877-294-5427
www.uncommonthread.com

Glossary

backstitch very strong hand stitch. Closely imitates machine stitching and is used to make a secure seam.

baste temporary means of holding fabric pieces together using large hand-sewn running stitches.

bias strip a strip of fabric cut diagonally across the grain of the fabric. It is used for bindings because it is stretchy and so will bend around curves and corners, unlike a straight-cut strip.

bodice front or back part of a garment, from the waist upward.

casing a narrow double hem at the wrist or ankle edge of a garment, used as a channel to take elastic, cord, or ribbon.

facing a means of finishing the edge of a neckline, armhole, or collar.

fuse term for fixing iron-on interfacing to the wrong side of a piece of fabric to be stiffened.

gathering stitch large machine stitch which creates gathers when drawn up. Used for sleeve caps and skirts, for example.

grain vertical or horizontal threads of a woven fabric.

hem/double hem a folded and stitched edge on part of a garment.

hook-and-loop fastener (velcro) synthetic closure in two parts, available in tape form or small dots. One side has small loops; the other side has small hooks, which stick to each other firmly when brought together.

iron-on interfacing nonwoven (usually) fabric that has adhesive on one side. Iron onto the wrong side of a fabric to create firmness, for hats, collars, cuffs, or facings.

leather punch hand tool used to make different-size holes in thick materials such as leather, fake leather, fabric, paper, or cardboard.

overlap topmost part of an opening or fastening.

presser foot a device screwed or clipped onto the sewing machine to hold the fabric in place under the needle. It is hinged to cope with fabrics of various thicknesses. Most machines will have several feet for different purposes, e.g., a zipper foot or buttonhole foot.

rickrack woven decorative braid in a zigzag shape.

running stitch a small regular hand stitch used for small seams.

seamline line at which two pieces of fabric are stitched together.

selvage woven edges of a fabric that run parallel with the vertical, warp, threads.

slipstitch small hand stitch used to close small openings in seams.

topstitch decorative stitching close to the edge of a collar or hemmed edge—can be in contrasting thread if desired.

undercollar underpart of a collar, to which the interfacing (if included) is usually fused.

underlap under part of an opening or fastening.

warp vertical, or lengthwise, threads of a woven fabric.

weft horizontal, or crosswise, threads of a woven fabric.

yoke top part of a garment, from which the rest hangs—the portion at the shoulder, for example.

Index

Acknowledgments

Dedicated to Tania.

The author would like to thank the owners of the all the fabulous dogs featured in this book.

IN ORDER OF APPEARANCE:

Jenny Milner and Archie

Christine Reynolds and Millie

Paul Manser and Smokey

Rosemary Parris and Red

Mandie Yaxley and Rolie

Tony Seddon and Spice

Richard Thorpe and Huxley

Mary Fossella and Domino and Disney

Tracy Potter and Eggs and Chips

Rachel Hartshorn and Charlie

Allison South and Yogi

Hazel Scott and Towser

Phil Jeffries and Knightsfollie Ladiesman (Mr. Jeffries)

Also a great big thank you to Anna, Clare, Caroline, and all at Ivy Press and Calvey and Paul "the dog whisperer" at the studio.

But I really wanted to be the fairy!

Well, I think that all went well, don't you?

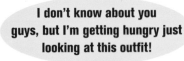

I don't know about you guys, but I'm getting hungry just looking at this outfit!

PHOTO CREDITS

The publisher wishes to thank the following for the use of pictures:

CORBIS 41 /Bob Krist, 49 /Bettmann, 67 /Hulton-Deutsch, 87 /Michael Prince, 93 /Neal Preston.